GW00891379

ECUMENICAL STUDIES IN HISTORY

No. 10

CHRISTIAN INITIATION

by

GEOFFREY WAINWRIGHT

LUTTERWORTH PRESS

LONDON

First published 1969

LUTTERWORTH PRESS
4 Bouverie Street, London, E.C.4

JOHN KNOX PRESS
RICHMOND, VIRGINIA, U.S.A.

7188 1385 5

Printed in Great Britain by
Latimer Trend & Co Ltd, Plymouth

CONTENTS

ECUMENICAL STUDIES IN HISTORY

The purpose of this series is to examine afresh problems of church history, and to do this for the sake of church unity. The subjects are drawn from many periods, places and communions. Their unity lies not in a common outlook of the writers, nor in a common method of treatment. It lies solely in the aim of, in one way or another, directly or indirectly, furthering the unity of the church. The contributors are no less diverse than the subjects, and represent many churches, nations and races.

INTRODUCTION

FOR THE PAST twenty-five years Christian initiation has been an important concern of theology, both in the academic and in the pastoral spheres. In Britain, the Church of England and the Church of Scotland have undertaken major re-examinations of their theology and practice of initiation.[1] Theologians and pastors have been equally concerned with a renewed understanding and practice of initiation in many other countries, particularly in western Europe. There is a twofold existential occasion for this interest: the movement towards Christian unity has revealed the need to establish a theology and a practice of initiation acceptable to the denominations at present divided on this as on other issues, and (perhaps even more urgently) the increasing breakdown of the *corpus christianum* is driving almost all denominations to rethink their customary practices of initiation so that they may better reflect the present relations between the Church and the world.

A great deal of work has been done on the problems of initiation, but often in isolation of country from country, denomination from denomination, pastor from academic, biblical exegete from dogmatician, liturgical scholar from pastoral theologian. There seemed room, therefore, for an overall survey such as the one which follows. More, it is hoped that by the way of ordering the multifarious material, by the running commentary on it and by the conclusions finally drawn from it, the present essay may itself be of some use in the general task of elaborating a pattern of initiation which is truly ecumenical: grounded in the Scriptures and in the Tradition of the Church—making for, and then acceptable in, a visibly united Church embracing all Christians—and serving the proclamation of the gospel by the now divided and then united Church for the establishment of God's kingdom in the whole world.

Despite the writer's ecumenical intention, it is inevitable that some will find statements in a study of this kind which they do not consider to represent accurately their own denominational position: in so far as this is due not to the variety of opinions which is found within the denominations themselves but rather to my inadequate empathy into other traditions than my own Methodist, I ask for pardon.

The study starts with the New Testament theology of initiation, and particularly as this is reflected in the work of biblical scholars in recent years. The next chapters deal in turn with the three main patterns of initiation which have been practised in Church history—the total initiation of infants (by baptism, "confirmation" and first communion), the pattern according to which baptism is given to infants while "confirmation" and first communion are reserved for later years, and "believers' baptism"; and in each case an evaluation of these patterns in their present circumstances is undertaken. The fifth chapter treats the relations between initiation and the unity of the Church from the viewpoints of theology, history and the contemporary movement towards churchly unity. The sixth is concerned with the role of initiation in the Church's participation in God's mission for the salvation of the world. In conclusion some consequences are drawn from the foregoing study for the elaboration of an ecumenical pattern of initiation.

ROME, ADVENT 1966* G.W.

* Literature noted after the completion of the manuscript includes: Th. Maertens, *Histoire et pastorale du rituel du catéchuménat et du baptême*, Bruges, 1962; W. Bieder, *Die Verheissung der Taufe im Neuen Testament*, Zürich, 1966; L. L. Mitchell, *Baptismal Anointing*, London, 1966; T. C. Akeley, *Christian Initiation in Spain c. 300–1100*, London, 1967; K. Aland, *Die Stellung der Kinder in den frühen christlichen Gemeinden—und ihre Taufe*, 1967; *La Maison-Dieu*, no. 89 (1967), which is devoted to infant baptism; the international Catholic periodical *Concilium* 3 (1967), no. 22 (February), which issue deals with questions of initiation; *Baptism and Confirmation: a Report submitted by the Church of England Liturgical Commission to the Archbishops of Canterbury and York December 1966*, London, 1967; *Entry into the Church*, services authorized for experimental use by the British Methodist Conference 1967; A. Aubry, "Faut-il re-baptiser? Enquête historique et interrogations théologiques" in *Nouvelle Revue Théologique* 89 (1967), pp. 183–201; a long book by the American Baptist, D. Moody, *Baptism: Foundation for Christian Unity*, Philadelphia, 1967; and the new R.C. rite of infant baptism, on which see B. Fischer in *Notitiae*, Città del Vaticano, 4 (1968), pp. 235–45.

I

THE NEW TESTAMENT THEOLOGY OF INITIATION

KARL BARTH's wartime attack on the baptizing of infants[1] provided a major stimulus for a fresh examination of the whole theology of baptism according to the New Testament. Future chapters will deal with the historical question of a primitive practice of infant baptism and with the theological issues concerning the rightness of its later practice. My present concern is to draw attention to the basic points in the total theology of baptism as these have been revealed by the scholarly scrutiny lavished on the New Testament texts in the last twenty years. This survey will itself be one measure of the ecumenical agreement on Christian initiation, for the academic work has been pursued by writers of many denominations. It will also indicate the fundamental theological *données* for the manner of whose doctrinal development and practical exercise we shall have to examine the Church of the past in its varying historical circumstances, if we wish to be pointed by the Bible and by ecclesiastical tradition to an ecumenical pattern of initiation which will be a fitting embodiment of the Gospel in our own situation.

It was in Switzerland that Barth exploded his bombshell; and Reformed theologians in that country, including Barth's own son, have played an important part in the New Testament investigation. In 1944, F. J. Leenhardt of Geneva published his *Le Baptême chrétien, son origine, sa signification,* in which he concluded that baptism is "le signe de ce que Dieu a fait en Christ pour les pécheurs; de ce qu'il veut donc faire par Christ dans le pécheur; de ce qu'il fait réellement lorsque la foi saisit son action et rencontre sa volonté gracieuse". O. Cullmann's *Die Tuaflehre des Neuen Testaments* appeared in 1948.[2] Markus Barth's *Die Tuafe—ein Sakrament?* (1951) challenged what he saw as the traditional sacramental understanding of baptism on the basis of a detailed study of the New Testament texts. Germany entered the lists in 1948–49, when H. W. Bartsch published *Die Taufe im Neuen Testament.* The English Methodist scholar, W. F. Flemington, published his *The New*

Testament Doctrine of Baptism in 1948. Two lengthy and learned works by British Baptist scholars have appeared more recently: R. E. O. White's *Biblical Doctrine of Initiation* (1960) and G. R. Beasley-Murray's *Baptism in the New Testament* (1962). The interpretation of the biblical data has not been neglected in the Anglican controversy about the reform of initiation practice; a fair part of G. W. H. Lampe's major work on the relation between baptism and confirmation, *The Seal of the Spirit* (1951), is devoted to the New Testament doctrine. The study of the German Catholic, R. Schnackenburg, *Das Heilsgeschehen bei der Taufe nach dem Apostel Paulus* (1950) won praise from many Protestants and has now been put into English by G. R. Beasley-Murray;[3] it is a profound study of baptism as "sacramental dying and rising with Christ". The Roman Catholic symposium *Baptism in the New Testament* (A. George *et al.*), which appeared in English translation in 1964, is composed of essays originally written for two issues of the Dominican periodical, *Lumière et Vie*, in 1956.

A striking feature of recent work is a renewed emphasis on Christ's own Baptism as a pointer to the understanding of Christian baptism. Its importance was appreciated by the early Christian artists, to judge by its popularity as a subject for painting and sculpture.[4] The Eastern Churches have never lost sight of this mystery of the life of Jesus Christ: it recurs in pictorial representation in their iconography, and it is celebrated every year in the great festival of the Epiphany. Christ's Baptism continued long as a favoured subject of Western artists (one thinks, for example, of the painting by Piero della Francesca now in the National Gallery, London, or of that by Andrea del Verrocchio now in the Uffizi), but Western theologians have largely neglected it as a clue to Christian baptism. Yet its vital importance for Christian baptism is illustrated by the fact that the Coptic Church calls its font *al-Urdunn*, the Jordan. Western theologians are now happily beginning to rediscover that Christ's experience at Jordan not only provides one of the historical bases for the practice of the Church from earliest days (a valuable basis because it gives dominical grounding to ecclesiastical baptism when many[5] are reluctant to accept Matt. 28: 19 as a *verbum Christi*) but also helps in the theological interpretation of Christian baptism.

Christ's Baptism was a prefiguration of the rest of His saving ministry. At Jordan He was declared to be the Son of God and the Servant of the Lord.[6] Jesus Himself was to refer to His coming death as a baptism (Mark 10: 38f.; Luke 12: 50),[7] so that His Baptism in water appears to have been a foreshadowing of the death on Calvary by which the righteous Servant of the Lord bore the sins of many and made many to be accounted righteous (cf. Isa. 53: 11–12).[8] When Jesus came up[9] from the waters of Jordan, there descended upon Him the Holy Spirit promised to the Messiah (Isa. 11: 2) and to the Servant (Isa. 42: 1), the Spirit whom Jesus received at His ascension to pour out on the Messianic people of the last days (Acts 2: 33).

Christian baptism reflects the pattern of Christ's Baptism, now applying to the individual the benefits won by the completed work of Christ; and like Christ's own Baptism it is both actual and proleptic in effect, a foreshadowing of the total process of which it is itself already a part. In Christian baptism one participates in the death and resurrection of Jesus Christ (Rom. 6; Col. 2: 11f.); one's sins are forgiven (Acts 2: 38), one is justified (1 Cor. 6: 11) on account of His righteousness; one is adopted as a son of God (Gal. 3: 26–4: 7; cf. Rom. 8: 12–17); one is anointed (2 Cor. 1: 21f.; 1 John 2: 20, 27) with the Spirit (Acts 2: 38; 1 Cor. 6: 11; 12: 13; 2 Cor. 1: 22) into the Messianic people (1 Cor. 12: 13; Gal. 3: 27–29); and all this with a view to the "day of redemption" (Eph. 4: 30; cf. John 3: 5).

Baptism is therefore, in Flemington's apt phrase, "the *kerygma* in action": it is the saving work of Christ preached and applied to the individual. A number of scholars[10] have in fact seen in this rich concept of baptism one mode of expressing a complete soteriology: Christ's Baptism at Jordan—the general baptism of all mankind (so Cullmann), or of the Church,[11] in the Representative on the Cross—the individual appropriation in Christian baptism.

Some recent Baptist writers, though holding to Christian baptism as participation in Christ's death and resurrection, have shown great suspicion of this presentation of a complete soteriology in baptismal terms.[12] It is a pity that they have been blinded to the merits of the prime argument by the fact that its proponents often take a much more debatable and far from self-evident second step and argue that just as Christ's original Baptism at Jordan and Calvary was accomplished independently of all men for whom it was undertaken, so also Christian baptism, as the sovereign act of God's grace which brings individuals to participation in that once-for-all saving event, is fitly administered prior to the individual's knowledge of what is happening, i.e. to infants.

It will be seen in chapter IV that Baptists can make a strong counter-argument to that second step, thus: as in Jesus's Baptism at Jordan and

Calvary there was human response to divine initiative, so the divine grace proclaimed in the *kerygma* must be met by the candidate's faith when Christian baptism is administered. Yet the prime insight into the relation among the baptisms at Jordan, Golgotha and the Christian font need not be obscured by the more doubtful conclusion drawn from it, nor should it be.

The Christological meaning of baptism carries with it also an ecclesiological meaning. For baptism εἰς Χριστόν makes a person a member of Christ's Body, the Church. The increasing recognition of this churchly dimension of baptism by Protestant scholars is part of their rediscovery of the corporate nature of the Church after a long period of false individualism within Protestantism. O. Cullman, for example, stresses (p. 32) that baptism is the divine "addition" (cf. προσετέθησαν at Acts 2: 41) of a new member to the Body of Christ. G. R. Beasley-Murray (p. 282) points out that the New Testament doctrine of baptism precludes any purely private relationship to Christ or any bestowal of the Spirit for purely private enjoyment in isolation from the Christian fellowship: "in one Spirit we were all baptized into one Body" (1 Cor. 12: 13), and baptism is the ground of fellowship in the Holy Spirit with Christ *and with His saints.*

When baptism is allowed its ecclesiastical character, its importance in the matter of Christian unity becomes clear. Those who have been baptized into Christ are all "one man (εἷς)" in Him, and there is neither Jew nor Greek, slave nor free, male nor female (Gal. 3: 27f.; cf. Col. 3: 9–11). There is but one baptism, just as there is one body, one Spirit, one hope, one Lord, one faith, and one God and Father of us all (Eph. 4: 4–6). In sharp words to the factious Corinthians Paul shows that schism is a Christological and baptismal absurdity: "Is Christ divided? Was Paul crucified for you? Or were you baptized in the name of Paul?" (see 1 Cor. 1: 10–17). The part which the theology and practice of baptism have actually been playing in the modern movement towards Church unity will be discussed in chapter V.

Because it introduces men into Christ and into the Church, baptism points to the End. J. Jeremias[13] has laid weight on the eschatological reference of the sacrament as making for a primitive practice of infant baptism: there would be no delay in ensuring the salvation of the whole family through incorporation into Christ and His Body in view of the imminent End. Whatever the value accorded to that inference in favour of infant baptism, it is increasingly recognized that for the New Testament writers baptism means the beginning of life in the Spirit, the first-fruits (Rom. 8: 23) and earnest (2 Cor. 1: 22; Eph. 1: 13f.) of the *eschaton*—otherwise the beginning of life in Christ, and "if any man is in Christ, καινὴ κτίσις" (2 Cor. 5: 17). In baptism, the Christian is sealed by the Holy Spirit unto a day of redemption (Eph. 4: 30). Without being born ἄνωθεν of water and the Spirit, no man may enter the Kingdom of God (John 3: 3–7).

Meanwhile, Christians have already to live according to the ethical implications of their baptism. Through having shared Christ's death and resurrection the baptized are henceforward dead to sin and alive to righteousness. The indicative is the basis for an imperative: Christians are to lay hold of what is already given to them, they are to become what they already are. "We were buried therefore with him by baptism into death, so that as Christ was raised from the dead by the glory of the Father, we too might walk in newness of life. . . . So you also must reckon yourselves dead to sin and alive to God in Christ Jesus. Let not sin therefore reign in your mortal bodies . . . but yield yourselves to God as men who have been brought from death to life, and your members to God as instruments of righteousness" (Rom. 6; cf. Col. 3: 1–15). Col. 3: 12–15 and Eph. 4 reveal that baptismal ethics are not a matter for the individual's conduct alone but concern the corporate life of the Church. Baptism into Christ is the ground of a united, loving and peaceful life together in His community.

On fundamental matters of the Christological, ecclesiological, eschatological and ethical meaning of baptism, there has been widespread agreement among recent New Testament scholars, whatever their denominational allegiance. Discord arises when the discussion turns to the question of grace and faith, to the working of God and man, in relation to baptism. Throughout the study in hand, this question will recur as an issue of ecclesiastical doctrine and practice affecting the ecumenical concerns of the Church's unity and mission. At this stage our direct business is with New Testament exegesis. It is apparent, however, that exegetes work within a confessional framework: in general the dividing lines between them in their scholarly work on this question coincide with the differences that exist among the baptismal doctrines and practices of their various churches.

When Markus Barth wrote *Die Taufe—ein Sakrament?*, he was a pastor of the Reformed Church in German-speaking Switzerland: his exegesis of the New Testament led him to stress baptism as a human act of obedience, an open declaration of faith in response to the deeds of

God already done; and this is not an unfamiliar emphasis in an area in which Zwingli's mark is stamped so deeply on the Church. (Already Dr Eck pointed out that Zwingli's "sacramental" theology brought him close to the very Anabaptists whom (for socio-political reasons) he was persecuting: Markus Barth has in fact now turned American Baptist.)

The Baptist scholars, White and Beasley-Murray, find that, on New Testament evidence, baptism, a work in which both God and man act, takes place only upon confession of faith. Standing in an "evangelical" Anglican tradition where "conversion" plays its part, C. F. D. Moule holds that the New Testament's doctrine of baptism is one that cannot be applied willy-nilly to the baptism of infants.[14] The similar conclusion of W. F. Flemington (p. 135) reflects a Methodist hesitation on the relation between baptism and conversion in the work of salvation that has been present from Wesley onwards.[15]

Heir to a covenantal theology in the Calvinist mould, O. Cullmann considers that baptism is first and foremost a saving act of grace in relation to which faith is a response and not a precondition: the baptism of the Mosaic Exodus was given to all (*πάντες*), though it did not suffice to save some (*τινες*) because they did not respond to it in faith (1 Cor. 10: 1ff.); first God acts in baptism, *and then* the baptized should understand his baptism and believe he has been saved (Rom. 6: 11); the confession of faith before baptism in the New Testament is to be taken as an indication of the divine will that the person be baptized, an indication which might also be provided by the fact of birth to Christian parents.

From an examination of the gospel miracle stories, J. Duplacy[16] discovers that the divine action may be preceded by the faith of others than the person directly concerned and may itself produce faith in the beneficiary, and he then applies this particular "structure of personal salvation" to the baptism of infants: and one remembers that Roman Catholic theologians, in the wake of Augustine (Ep. 98; PL 33, 359–64), are accustomed to justify infant baptism on the bases of *fides aliena* (of Church and sponsors) and of the notion that the "sacrament of faith" actually *makes* the child a believer.

The New Testament seems to favour now one, now another view of the relation between grace and faith in baptism, and sometimes the same passage is made to support opposing positions. Is it possible that the scholars are making upright but *mistaken* attempts to find a uniformity among texts which are genuinely divergent? Is the New Testament pattern one of a diversity in baptismal practice which reflects the rich variety of God's dealings with men and embodies more clearly now one, now another aspect of the fundamental mystery of the divine work of bringing men to salvation? Can it therefore be that the variety of positions adopted within and among the churches today is biblically justified? Will the One Church see several positions continue to be maintained, viewed as complementing each other rather than as mutually exclusive, with the circumstances in which the Church lives and prosecutes its mission determining the predominant practice in each situation?

Before leaving the question of the New Testament basis of baptismal theology and practice, it is important to take note of the imagery used in connection with the sacrament. For verbal, material and dramatic symbols are indispensable parts of the baptismal act; and our attention to biblical and ecclesiastical tradition in this matter may help towards the discovery of words, things and actions which not only are true to the given content and expression of the sacrament but also make possible a striking communication of its meaning in the cultural situations of today. The symbol will be at its best when it is at one and the same time rooted in elementary human thought and behaviour, sanctified by the usage of Bible and Church, and in touch with the particular geographical and social environment in which it is employed.

At its simplest baptism involves:

(*a*) The pronouncement of the divine Name. A simple Christological style may perhaps have been in use in the primitive Church (cf. Acts 2: 38; 8: 16, 37; 10: 48; 19:5; Rom. 10: 9), but it was the Trinitarian, present at Matt. 28: 19, which gained the day. At an early date this part of baptism seems in some cases at least, to have consisted of the candidate's giving an affirmative answer, while standing in the water, to the minister's questions whether he believed in each of the Three Persons of the Trinity;[17] but later usage, possibly on account of the growing preponderance of infant candidates who could not themselves answer the questions, settled for a direct pronouncement by the minister: "N., I baptize thee in the Name (of the Trinity)" or "N. is baptized in the Name (of the Trinity)."[18]

(*b*) The water. In biblical imagery, as elsewhere, water is the ambivalent symbol of destruction and new life, besides possessing purificatory significance from its use in washing; the Bible also associates the Spirit with water. Hence the appropriateness of water in the sacrament of death and resurrection with Christ,[19] cleansing from sin and bestowal of the Spirit.

(*c*) The act of dipping the baptizand under the water, or of pouring it or sprinkling it upon him. A. Stenzel[20] doubts whether complete submersion was the invariable method in New Testament times, since it is by no means clear that facilities would always be readily available for this in the early missionary period (see, e.g., Acts 2: 41; 16: 30ff.). Theodore of Mopsuestia describes the minister as placing his hand on the candidate's head and thrice ducking him completely under the water in which he stood;[21] but another early type of practice may be reflected in some of the catacomb pictures of Christ's Baptism, which show Him standing more or less waist-deep in the water with water being poured over His head and momentarily enveloping Him. Stenzel believes that this second style is sufficient to account for the use of words like *baptizare*, *mergere* and *tingere* in the Fathers, and accords well with the shallowness of most of the fonts unearthed by archaeologists. The modes of baptism have been a matter of dispute among the churches: the Orthodox have objected to the Western use of sprinkling (and even affusion, except in an emergency), and Baptists have usually held complete submersion to be the only right method.

The word, the water and the action are generally regarded by the churches as the irreducible elements in the rite of baptism; but the New Testament knows various baptismal images which have been the subject of further liturgical development in different ages and places:

1. Baptism means change of ownership and allegiance. The baptized person is no longer a slave to sin but a slave to God (Rom. 6). Baptism "into the name of" Christ transfers a man "into His ownership". One of the ideas attaching to the term "seal" (cf. 2 Cor. 1: 21–22; Eph. 1: 13–14; 4: 30) is that of the marking of property; and in the patristic period "sealing" commonly means the tracing of the sign of the Cross on the forehead in oil after baptism, marking the baptized person for Christ as a slave was branded for his owner and a soldier tattooed for his emperor. The Oriental rites dramatized this transfer of allegiance from Satan to Christ in a ceremony just before the actual baptism: in his *apotaxis* from Satan the candidate turned to the West, the place of darkness, and renounced him, even spitting on him in some rites; then he turned eastwards, towards the light, and professed his *syntaxis* to Christ his new Lord. In the Western rites the renunciation of the devil was matched by the baptismal confession itself as the acknowledgment of the divine Lordship.[22]

2. Baptism means to strip off "the old man" and to don "the new man" who is Christ (Col. 3: 9–10; Gal. 3: 27). Undressing and dressing

before and after baptism acquire a symbolic meaning. The clothing of the newly baptized in white garments is attested by Cyril of Jerusalem and by Ambrose;[23] it still takes place in most of the Oriental rites and is vestigially present in the Roman. The Church of South India has provided for its optional use in believers' baptism.

3. Baptism is birth to new life (John 3: 5; Titus 3: 5–7). The shape of the Christian font is often suggestive of the womb.

4. Baptism is enlightenment (Heb. 6: 4; 10: 32; cf. 1 Pet. 2: 9). The Western custom of giving a lighted taper to the newly baptized persists in the Roman rite and has been adopted for optional use by the Church of South India. At the Easter vigil service in the Roman Catholic Church the renewal of baptismal vows[24] is preceded by the lighting of a candle by each of the faithful from the great paschal candle.

5. Baptism makes a person a sharer in Christ, the anointed King and Priest (note the word-play in 2 Cor. 1: 21; cf. 1 Pet. 2: 9; Rev. 1: 6; 5: 10). The development of post-baptismal anointing is a complicated story, but there is no doubt that a part was played in it by the idea of participation in the Christ.[25]

6. Hebrew kings and high priests wore crowns (*nēzer*), and Greek victors received wreaths. Christians can look forward to their coronation (1 Cor. 9: 25; 2 Tim. 4: 8; Jas. 1: 12; 1 Pet. 5: 4; Rev. 2: 10), and this is anticipated in a post-baptismal ceremony of crowning in the Oriental rites apart from the Byzantine.[26]

Many of these symbols accompanying baptism, based on biblical imagery and long practised in the Church, may still speak to the elemental human condition at a subconscious level, as well as providing didactic and parenetic opportunities. But may they not be supplemented by others more closely in touch with the particular forms of civilization today? Is advancing technology producing things which could become universally understood baptismal symbols? Have Asia and Africa indigenous symbols fit for use in the baptismal practice of the Church in those continents?

Confirmation in the New Testament?

The debates on the relation between baptism and confirmation that have been taking place in the Roman Catholic and Anglican Churches in particular have driven the scholars to consult the New Testament texts. One often gains the impression, however, that in this matter, as with the exegesis of verses concerning the relation between grace and faith in the baptismal event, the interpretation of vexed passages is governed by a theological *parti pris*.

In the Anglican sphere the characteristic controversy was that sparked off by Dom Gregory Dix's Oxford lecture on *The Theology of Confirmation in relation to Baptism*;[27] a number of articles appeared in the monthly *Theology* before G. W. H. Lampe published his lengthy refutation of Dix's position in *The Seal of the Spirit* (London, 1951); L. S. Thornton countered with *Confirmation: its Place in the Baptismal Mystery* (London, 1954) which was dedicated to the memory of Dix; Lampe reasserted his view in several articles and exercised a strong influence on the World Council of Churches' Faith and Order report on *The Meaning of Baptism*.[28]

The position held, with some variations, by both Dix and Thornton was roughly this: already in New Testament times "baptism" was a complex whole comprising water baptism *and* either the imposition of hands or chrismation or both, the single term "baptism" sometimes being used *pars pro toto*. Each part of the rite had its own meaning and effect: water baptism conferred forgiveness of sins and regeneration, and the laying on of hands or chrismation bestowed the indwelling Spirit. The sacraments of baptism and confirmation are supposed to be the parts into which the Western Church has separated this original baptismal whole, and the conclusion is at hand that those who have been baptized but not confirmed have not received the sacramental gift of the indwelling Spirit.

Realizing the implications for the ecumenical movement of a view which denies that the unconfirmed are fully initiated Christians, Lampe sought to prove that, according to the New Testament, baptism in water provided complete initiation and conferred all the benefits of salvation, of which the indwelling of the Holy Spirit was one. The other ceremonies which attached themselves to baptism in the early Church were simply edifying symbols underscoring some of the aspects of salvation already bestowed in the water baptism itself.

Among Roman Catholic scholars there is, as will be seen in a later chapter, a marked difference of emphasis between those who regard the present sacrament of confirmation as the completing "seal" of the initiation begun in baptism and those who stress rather the independence of the sacrament of confirmation as a "strengthening for the fight"; but this division is not much reflected in their interpretation of New Testament evidence concerning what is for Anglicans the key question of the sacramental bestowal of the Holy Spirit.

There are probably two reasons for the greater unanimity among the Catholics at this point: the larger part allowed to later ecclesiastical development in the making of doctrine in the Catholic Church means that the theologians do not feel so obliged to find their particular view of the sacraments already present in detail in the New Testament texts; and the fact that received Catholic doctrine holds baptism itself to be in the last resort sufficient sacramental bestowal of salvation means that a decisive role must be accorded to the Spirit in baptism, whatever further role may be assigned to Him in confirmation.

At this stage I simply indicate the more important New Testament evidence which has figured in the debate on the relation between baptism and confirmation:

1. It has been argued that the phraseology of such texts as Acts 2: 38 and Titus 3: 5 indicates that there were two moments in the primitive initiation: the gift of the Spirit was not the internal accompaniment of the external baptism in water but came rather through a separate ceremony *after* water baptism.[29] Against this interpretation of Acts 2: 38[30] it may be urged that a similar syntactical construction in Acts 16: 31 suggests that Luke meant Peter to promise a reception of the Holy Spirit which was contemporaneous with baptism for the remission of sins. In Titus 3: 5, the interpretation depends on how one construes a string of Greek genitives (ἔσωσεν ἡμᾶς διὰ λουτροῦ παλιγγενεσίας καὶ ἀνακαινώσεως Πνεύματος Ἁγίου): *either* "the bath of regeneration" and "the renewal of the Holy Spirit" are two distinct events *or* "regeneration" and "renewal" describe a single reality effected by the Holy Spirit at "the bath".

2. Though a few deny that the sealing with the Spirit mentioned in 2 Cor. 1: 22, Eph. 1: 13; 4: 30 has any reference at all to an external rite, most recent scholars are agreed that this sealing with the Spirit is related to the baptismal event. On the ground that the "sealing" in the *Apostolic Tradition* of Hippolytus took place at the episcopal anointing rather than at the water baptism, Dix held that the New Testament texts refer to that part of the initiation rite which became "confirmation". While agreeing that the signing of the cross on the forehead in oil came to be one of the common meanings of "sealing" in the patristic period,[31] Lampe argued that the New Testament is to be interpreted in the light of the earlier usage which make baptism in water the sacramental medium of the seal of the Spirit; this meaning is found in Hermas, *Simil.* 9, 16 (PG 2, 995–96), and it also persisted alongside the other meanings attested later. In the face of this evidence that there can

be no assumption of a simple equivalence between "seal" and "confirmation" in the early Church, Thornton continued to assert that, despite alternative uses of the word, the meaning of "seal" as "confirmation" had an unbroken ancestry reaching back into the New Testament; but it remains that no one has in fact been able to find, apart from precisely the disputed cases in the New Testament, an instance of this usage much before the end of the second century.

3. Dix, among others, wished to see evidence of an anointing ceremony in the use of *χρίω* at 2 Cor. 1: 21 and *χρῖσμα* at 1 John 2: 20, 27. Though the idea of Christians as the anointed ones lent itself to expression in an outward ceremony, most scholars are reluctant to place the beginning of the use of physical anointing in the initiation rite as early as New Testament times.[32] Dix received support, however, from the unexpected quarter of Presbyterianism in an article by T. W. Manson.[33] On the basis of 1 John 2: 20 the writer considered it feasible that a physical anointing for the sacramental gift of the Spirit formed part of an initiation rite which he found reflected in 1 John 5: 8: the Spirit, the water and the blood match the gift of the Spirit (possibly by laying on of hands and anointing), baptism in water, and the first communion.[34] Dix had already argued for this order of events as a primitive order; some early Syrian rites[35] certainly have the order: anointing—water baptism—eucharist; and Dix believed that here was a primitive Christian practice which followed the order of events in Jewish proselyte initiation: the "seal" of circumcision—baptism—sacrifice.

4. The scholars who hold that the imposition of hands formed part of the primitive rite of initiation appear to stand on fairly safe ground. It is now frequently accepted that this was so at least in the circles known to the Writer to the Hebrews (see 6: 2). But it is by no means agreed that the incidents in Acts 8: 14ff.; 19: 5f., prove that the laying on of hands was the normal medium for the conferring of the Spirit in the primitive rite.[36] Lampe argued that this opinion stems from an erroneous interpretation of the texts which is not found before the end of the second century; the two incidents in Acts are rather to be seen as exceptional cases in which a special ceremony of acceptance into the fellowship of the apostolic Church marked a crucial point in the spread of the mission. G. R. Beasley-Murray[37] considers it inconceivable that the Samaritans should have been baptized in the name of Jesus and *not* have received the Spirit, and interprets Acts 8: 17 as the impartation rather of His special charismata in which Luke showed much interest. The same scholar believes that the Ephesian incident as a whole bears

the stamp of an exceptional event, though he leaves open the possibility that despite the silence in his letters Paul may have used the laying on of hands at the administration of baptism in the name of Jesus on other occasions besides that recorded in Acts 19: 5f.; where such an action took place at baptism it must be interpreted as an underlining of the bestowal of the Spirit already inherent in baptism itself. The most common Roman Catholic view is that represented by B. Neunheuser:[38] in the normal New Testament rite of initiation there were two moments, baptism in water and the laying on of hands; there was an initial mediation of the Spirit in the former, and a complementary in the latter.

5. Some scholars turn to the patterns of major events in salvation history for support of their opinion that baptism and confirmation represent two distinct stages in the one total action of initiation. These scholars follow a line of interpretation which is not uncommon among the Fathers[39] when they distinguish two moments in the Baptism of Jesus: His Baptism in the water and the *subsequent* descent of the Spirit.[40] Another favourite theme is to make baptism correspond to the Death and Resurrection of Easter and confirmation to the Descent of the Holy Spirit at Pentecost.[41]

Where the old initiation rite continues to be celebrated as a single whole this question of the significance of its various parts is not so acute; but the Western development of the post-baptismal ceremonies into the separate sacrament of confirmation administered almost always at a considerable interval in time from the water baptism has called Western theologians to attempt some more definite explanation of the relation between the two. In chapter III we shall look at the historical development in the West and at the ways in which the modern theologians see the relation between baptism and confirmation at the present day; first, however, we examine the Churches in which a complex rite of inititiation is adminstered all at once.

II

INITIATION ANCIENT AND EASTERN

IT IS CERTAIN that the baptism of infants was practised in North Africa in Tertullian's time, and in Caesarea when Origen was in that city.[1] There is therefore no reason to discount the evidence of the *Apostolic Tradition*[2] when it records that children not of an age to answer for themselves were intitiated along with adults in a single rite in Rome at the beginning of the third century; even though Hippolytus's work may well have undergone considerably later revision before finding its way into any of the versions and adaptations, whether Latin or Oriental, now extant. Variations in practice are attested for different geographical areas,[3] but there are so many supporting witnesses[4] for so much of the rite of the *Apostolic Tradition* that an account of that rite will give a fair indication of the practice of the Church in the formative period of the third and fourth centuries.[5]

Tertullian states that Easter was the pre-eminent time for baptism, and it seems certain that the rite described in the *Apostolic Tradition* was celebrated during Easter night. Baptism was preceded by a long period of preparation. On being brought forward by sponsors those who sought entry into the Church were examined concerning their reasons for coming and their readiness to abandon evil ways and forbidden occupations. If found worthy, they were admitted to a catechumenate which, at least in Hippolytus's day, usually lasted three years. During this time they received instruction in classes which concluded with prayer and with a laying on of hands by the teacher. When they were "chosen"[6] to receive baptism, their sponsors had to testify that they had lived piously while catechumens. Then throughout their proximate preparation for baptism they were exorcized daily.[7] On the Thursday before baptism the candidates washed themselves; on the next two days they fasted. On the Saturday they received the final exorcism from the bishop, who also "breathed on their faces and sealed their foreheads and ears and noses". In the paschal vigil the candidates heard the Scriptures read and received instruction.

Baptism took place away from the full assembly, and in the following manner. At cock-crow prayer was said over the water. Having stripped, each candidate professed his renunciation of Satan and was anointed with the oil of exorcism (exorcized by the bishop), the administering presbyter saying, "Let all evil spirits depart from thee." Then the candidate went down into the water. He replied, "I believe", to each of three credal questions concerning the Trinity and was "baptized" by the minister (whether bishop or presbyter or deacon) upon each answer. On leaving the water the candidate was anointed by a presbyter with the oil of thanksgiving (previously consecrated by the bishop), the accompanying words being "I anoint thee with holy oil in the name of Jesus Christ". The newly-baptized dressed themselves and entered the full assembly. There the bishop laid hand upon them[8] and prayed.[9] Next he anointed the head of each one by hand, saying, "I anoint thee with holy oil in God the Father Almighty and Christ Jesus and the Holy Spirit." Then the bishop "sealed"[10] him on the forehead and gave him the kiss of peace.

Thereupon the neophytes enjoyed their new privileges as members of the Church: they joined in the prayers of the faithful, they shared the congregational kiss of peace, and they participated in the eucharistic liturgy proper. At their first communion the neophytes not only received the bread and wine but also partook of a cup of water and a cup of milk and honey.[11] The water is said to be an inward washing corresponding to the outward baptism, and the milk and honey is referred to the promise made to the Patriarchs concerning the promised land.

The only[12] churches whose usual practice is still to administer this total pattern of baptism, "confirmation" and first communion on the one occasion are churches in which, for reasons that will appear later, the infant initiation of children of Christian parents is the heavily preponderant practice and the initiation of an adult convert from outside the Christian sphere is a rarity.

Here are two or three examples of rites which were first fashioned for adults and which are now usually employed for infants:

1. The Byzantine rite begins with "prayers for a catechumen". After silent insufflations and consignations, the priest lays hand upon the person's head and says a prayer which appears to be for the making of a catechumen; then the Devil is summoned to come out and God is prayed to expel all evil spirits from the candidate and to make him a worthy member of the Church and an heir to the Kingdom. Thereupon the priest turns the candidate westwards and asks three times,

"Dost thou renounce Satan . . . ?" Each time the catechumen, or his sponsor ('Ἀνάδοχος), replies "I renounce". The priest asks thrice, "Hast thou renounced Satan?" and thrice the catechumen or his sponsor replies, "I have renounced". Next, the priest orders him to exhale and to spit on Satan. Having turned the candidate eastwards, the priest asks thrice, "Dost thou join thyself to Christ?" and "Hast thou joined thyself to Christ?"; the catechumen or sponsor answers appropriately and adds that he believes in Him as King and God. The candidate or sponsor recites the Nicene Creed and, having thrice more replied that he has adhered to Christ, bows down before the Trinity.

At the beginning of baptism the priest censes the font. A diaconal litany of intercession covers an *apologia sacerdotis* said quietly. Then the priest prays aloud to the Father for the sanctification of the water by the Holy Spirit, continuing, "And give it the grace of redemption, the blessing of Jordan. Make it the fountain of incorruption, the gift of holiness, the remission of sins . . ."; the priest signs the water thrice with the cross, breathing on it, and says thrice, "Let all adverse powers be crushed beneath the sign of Thy precious Cross . . .". After this prayer for the consecration of the water, the priest breathes thrice upon olive oil which the deacon brings to him, signs it thrice with the cross, and prays for God's blessing upon it. While a threefold Alleluia is sung, the priest then pours oil into the water crosswise. Next, the priest makes a cruciform anointing on the baptizand's forehead, breast, shoulders, ears, feet and hands, beginning with the words, "The servant of God, N., is anointed with the oil of gladness, in the name (of the Trinity)." Facing the east and holding the candidate upright, the priest then immerses him three times in the water, saying, "The servant of God, N., is baptized in the name (of the Trinity)". Thereupon Psalm 32 is sung, and the priest dresses the newly-baptized in the white garment, saying, "The servant of God, N., is clothed with the tunic of righteousness, in the name (of the Trinity)".

The priest says a prayer preparatory to chrismation. Chrismation takes place with the holy *myron*, a perfumed oil consecrated by the patriarch. The priest anoints the baptized with *myron* crosswise on the various parts of the body beginning with the forehead, saying, "The seal of the gift of the Holy Spirit. Amen." Then the priest, the sponsor and the baptized process round the font while "As many as have been baptized into Christ have put on Christ: Alleluia" is sung.

The concluding reading of the Apostle (Rom. 6: 3–11) and Gospel (Matt. 28: 16–20) betrays the fact that the eucharistic liturgy used to be taken up at this point. Nowadays, however, the neophyte's first communion is delayed until the following Sunday, unless he communicates at once from wine kept from a celebration of the liturgy before the baptism.

Two ceremonies which were formerly carried out a week after baptism are now attached directly to the baptismal service. The first is ablution: water is sprinkled on the baptismal dress, and the neophyte himself is sprinkled with water and washed with a sponge; at this removal of the material traces of his initiation, the candidate is assured that its spiritual effects are lasting, "Thou wast baptized, thou wast illumined, etc." The second ceremony is peculiar to the Byzantine rite: the cruciform cutting of the neophyte's hair by the priest; this is a sign that the baptized person is dedicated to God's glory.

2. The Coptic and Ethiopic rites[13] resemble one another very closely in structure and even in wording. The ceremonies of the catechumenate include the asking of the candidate's name and an anointing with plain oil ("May this oil bring to nought all the attacks of the adversary"). The ceremonies belonging more immediately before baptism proper comprise an imposition of hand, with prayer for deliverance from Satan, the candidate's renunciation of Satan,[14] an exorcistic insufflation (in the Coptic), his adhesion to Christ,[14] his profession of faith according to a brief Trinitarian formula,[14] and prayer for his strengthening. Then comes an anointing of the whole body in the oil of gladness (previously consecrated by the patriarch) followed by more prayers for the candidate (with imposition of hand in the Coptic). At this point in the Coptic rite plain oil is poured into the water.

Both rites continue with the Apostle (Titus 2: 11–3: 7), the Catholicon (1 John 5: 5–13), the Praxis (Acts 8: 26–39), the Psalm (Psalm 32: 1f.), the Gospel (John 3: 1–21) and the intercessions, as in the eucharistic rite. Then there are prayers for the baptizand and an *apologia sacerdotis*; three solemn prayers (for peace, the patriarch, and the congregation) and the recitation of the creed follow, again as in the eucharistic liturgy. Oil is poured into the water (plain oil in the Ethiopic, the oil of gladness in the Coptic). Next comes the great prayer for the blessing of the water, accompanied by insufflations and consignations and followed by the pouring of chrism (previously consecrated by the patriarch) into the water while Alleluia is sung.

Baptism is by trine immersion, with the active formula. There is a prayer for the deconsecration of the water. The forehead, and then the whole body, is anointed with chrism (". . . an unction of the grace of the Holy Spirit . . ."); and then there is an imposition of hand with prayer ("... Receive the Holy Spirit ..."; the Coptic has an insufflation at this point). In both rites the neophyte is then dressed in white, crowned and girdled. He communicates in wine and (in the Ethiopic only) receives milk and honey. Communion is followed by a prayer with imposition of hand, a benediction, and a hymn. The Copts take the neophyte in procession round the church while the hymn is sung.[15]

It is not easy to find a modern theological statement explaining how such a rite of total initiation, clearly composed with responsible subjects in mind, may properly be administered to infants. For the practice of giving total initiation to infants is confined to the Eastern Churches;[16] and these are churches which simply *do* things, without feeling the need of a neat rationale for them. On asking the question "Do all Christian parents have their infants baptized?" one is apt to receive the simple, possibly *simpliste*, reply, "Of course; otherwise the infants would not be Christians." The more analytical theologians of the West find themselves accused of leading into heresy through asking too many questions. Nevertheless we cannot renounce our Western birthright; and so theologize we must.

The churches which practise the complete initiation of infants are living in one of two historical situations: either they are found in countries where church and society are considered practically coterminous; or else they exist as well-defined, closely knit communities in a hostile or indifferent environment.

The Orthodox Churches in Greece and Ethiopia are the best remaining examples of the first type. The Orthodox Greek is both a churchman and a citizen, and in that order: the Greek father takes with him the ecclesiastical certificate of baptism when he visits the village mayor or the town hall for the civil registration of his child's birth. In Ethiopia, Christianity is the imperial religion, and whole tracts of the country are solidly Christian.

There are more instances of churches in the second type of situation. In India, the Jacobites are surrounded by Hindus and Buddhists; in Egypt, the Coptic Christians live in the midst of Islam. The Orthodox Churches of Eastern Europe live in communist countries whose governments and populaces show them varying degrees of hostility or indifference. The Orthodox Churches in Western Europe and North America are set within a pluralistic society tolerant of those of any religion and those of none; these churches are almost entirely composed of *émigrés* who have remained close together in their national socio-religious communities.

It is in these two types of situation that the administration of total Christian initiation to infants can, in fact, find its best rationale. In Greece, for instance, Christianity has been so much a part of the national life that the child has accompanied his parents in their more or less regular attendance at worship and has thereby learnt his faith gradually in the school of the liturgy. The Greek child receives, in addition, two hours of Christian teaching each week at day school. So he has stayed throughout his life in the church into which he was initiated as an infant. In countries in which the Orthodox Church is, for whatever reasons, sharply distinguished from its environment, its members have from the beginning of their lives been steeped in the worship and communal life which are its distinguishing features, and they have continued as the Orthodox Christians they were baptized. When, as in these circumstances, it is self-evident that a person will live his whole life as a Christian, then there is a case to be made for his total initiation at the very beginning.

There is no doubt, however, that the advance of a technological civilization is sweeping away the social patterns with which the life of these churches has been closely associated. Industry draws the Indian Jacobite from his village home into urban areas, and he finds himself alone and severed from the communal life of his church. The young Russian Orthodox is subjected to the pressures, whether crude or subtle, of atheism by the state; and the second and third generations of Orthodox immigrants in the U.S.A. take an increasing part in a more uniform American way of life, so that the Christian influence of the separated communities to which their fathers kept grows less and less, and they may drift from the faith altogether. The Greek in Athens and the Cypriot shop-owner in Liverpool alike find that affluence tends to reduce their participation in Christian worship.

Some churches are still barely affected by this movement, but it is clear that most of the Eastern Churches are beginning to have to face the same social factors that have confronted the Western Churches from the start of the modern industrial era. It will be interesting to see whether the different ethos of these churches leads them to tackle the problems on other lines than those tried by the Western Churches. One of the questions which they must bring themselves to ask, so it seems to me as a Western Protestant, is this: Is it right to continue the initiation of infants when it grows more and more uncertain whether they will stay in the Church?

Even where the circumstances are most favourable to the growth of the child in the Christian faith, the practice of administering total initiation to infants still raises all at once the various theological issues which bother many Protestants concerning the suitability of children as sacramental subjects. One such issue is the relation between baptism and the remission of sins. Baptism is "unto remission of sins" (Acts 2: 38): how does this apply to infants?

Many scholars consider that the notion of infants as embroiled in "original sin" played some part in the consolidation of the practice of infant baptism at least, if not in its origin. On the ground, however, that the Augustinian version of the doctrine of original sin, being unpalatable to "modern man", is false, G. R. Beasley-Murray[17] holds that baptism administered to infants cannot be true baptism because it cannot be unto remission of sins, there being nothing to remit.

But even if some theologians (with Beasley-Murray and against Augustine) are no longer willing to apply the strict language of sin and guilt before an age of "individual responsibility", the Christian view that a person shares from the beginning of his life in a fallen human nature which is turned in upon itself holds good—and indeed has received support from the psychological insights of "modern man" into the egocentricity of the infant. May not, therefore, the baptism of an infant be seen, even where there is a refusal to attach the categories of sin and guilt to the infant's solidarity with the human race "in Adam", as the proleptic remission, for Christ's sake, of the actual and culpable sins which the person will commit when at an age of responsibility he deliberately makes Adam's sin his own (as he certainly will)?

A more general and more important issue is that of the relation between the bestowal, not of forgiveness alone, but of any other benefit at all and the faith of the recipient of a sacrament. The baptismal rites outlined in this chapter envisage the case in which a responsible person is instructed in the faith, renounces Satan, and professes his allegiance to Christ and his faith in the Trinity—and yet they are administered to infants.

The Eastern Churches do not seem worried by this, nor has the Roman seemed to be by a similar state of affairs in its own rite of infant baptism;[18] but many Protestants in churches which practise infant baptism consider that the Baptist position has merit at least in so far as it springs from the desire to avoid a mechanical or magical view of the sacrament, and that they themselves must therefore demonstrate some connection between the baptism of infants and faith.

Recent Protestant apologetic for infant baptism has stressed the presence of faith in the baptizing Church and in the parents or other sponsors of the infant baptized. It is certainly true that every baptism is the occasion of the Church's witnessing to its faith; and the infant is certainly favoured who is born to faithful parents and committed to people who hold themselves bound to provide for his upbringing in the faith. Valuable though these ideas are, I would nevertheless maintain, at the risk of calling forth a disparaging reference to Renaissance individualism,[19] that the faith which finally matters in relation to baptism is the faith of the very person baptized. There are three possible ways of seeing the relation between baptism and personal faith in the case of those baptized as infants:

1. That the infant already has faith before baptism. This is the logical implication of the Eastern and Roman rites (and of Luther's *Taufbüchlein*) in which the questions are directly addressed to the infant and the sponsor replies simply as his mouthpiece, as though the candidate were a responsible person who either was dumb or did not understand the particular language of the rite.[20]

2. That faith is given at and through baptism itself. This is the theological view which prevailed, for example, in Lutheran orthodoxy and which is maintained in the Roman Catholic Church. (Both 1 and 2 have difficulty in withstanding the two tests which are normally applied to facts of faith: Few modern exegetes would accept Luther's view[21] that the leaping of the unborn John in Elizabeth's womb at Mary's Visitation (Luke 1: 41) was *biblical* proof that any infant might be expected to respond in faith when confronted by the Word of God; and (from the standpoint of *the Church's experience*) alongside those baptized in infancy who later come to profess their faith there must be set both those who, though baptized, never come to this profession and also those previously unbaptized who come to faith.)

3. That infants are baptized with a view to their future faith. Among the earlier rites there is an isolated case of this in the Bobbio Missal (*circa* A.D. 700) in which the sponsor replies "May he renounce" and "May he believe".[22] There is at least a hint at the idea in the address to the godparents in the 1662 *Book of Common Prayer* of the Church of England, even though the godparents are called upon to speak meanwhile in the name of the child.[23] The rite proposed by the Church of England's Liturgical Commission in 1958 retained the "I believe" spoken by the sponsors in the name of the child (to whom the interrogations are addressed). But many other modern Protestant services[24] ask the

parents or sponsors rather for a promise to provide such an upbringing for the infant that he may come to profess his own faith.

In churches where this is the use there is also a service, sometimes called confirmation, for the public profession of faith in later years, and this can be looked upon as the solemn occasion on which the person baptized as an infant completes on his part[25] the act which on God's part was completed in principle at the moment of baptism.[26] And, even in churches where it is held that sacramental grace is bestowed in it, confirmation may be understood as being, when administered at a later age to those baptized as infants, at least in part a solemn profession of faith.[27]

Those confirmed in infancy do not have this solemn single moment for the profession of their faith; but in the Eastern Churches the Blessing of the Waters at Epiphany as a memorial of Christ's Baptism affords an annual memorial of every baptism,[28] and all Roman Catholics have the opportunity to renew their baptismal vows at the paschal vigil every year. For all churches, moreover, the eucharistic liturgy offers a regular occasion for the profession of faith.

The question of *infants* and communion, however, is yet another theological issue raised by the administration of the total pattern of initiation to infants. Protestant churches which baptize infants, and often their theologians who are the most ardent defenders of this practice, nevertheless balk the giving of communion to infants; nor is infant communion common in the Roman Church. To the charge of inconsistency, often levelled by Baptists and their sympathizers against those who give baptism and deny communion to infants, Cullmann replies[29] by asserting that the eucharist is for those who already believe "to the exclusion of . . . the not-yet-believing", but he does not in fact make clear *why* those who have, on his own argument, been accepted, by God's gracious act in the baptism given to them as infants before they have faith, into the Body of Christ should not then just as well participate in the continuing life of the Church in the eucharist before they come to faith.[30] An American Lutheran,[31] on the other hand, has argued that the gospel of free grace calls for communion as well as baptism to be given to infants.

In fact, however, the whole of the Western Church inherits the Western medieval refusal of communion to infants; the process by which first communion became separated from baptism and confirmation will be narrated in the next chapter as part of the broader story of the disintegration of the initiation complex.

III

INITIATION MEDIEVAL AND WESTERN

THE Roman Catholic Church and (apart from the Baptist movement) the Churches of the Reformation alike stand heir to the development in the medieval West whereby baptism remained practised in infancy, while both "confirmation" and first communion came to be administered usually only after an interval of several years. From this standpoint Western theologians often tend towards the attitude that the Eastern Churches need to justify themselves for their practice of giving the complete initiation to infants. *Granted the rightness of infant baptism*, however, it is rather the West which must justify its own disruption of the full rite of initiation which was anciently administered at a single celebration, whether to adults or to infants. What precisely are the advantages of delaying "confirmation" (however understood) and communion in the case of those baptized in infancy?

It is with this question in mind that we now examine both the historical development in the West (in liturgy, theology and pastoral discipline) and also the present practice and understanding of the Churches which inherit that history.

As to *liturgical* history, there is good documentation for baptism and the post-baptismal ceremonies in Rome, but reconstruction of the practice in other parts of the West is made uncertain by considerable gaps in the evidence and by difficulties in its interpretation.[1] In all parts of the West, sponsors acted for the infants in the baptismal renunciations and profession of faith, and all the ceremonies of the catechumenate came to be performed together immediately before baptism. In Rome, the baptism and a first post-baptismal anointing could be performed by presbyters, but they were followed by a hand-laying (with prayer invoking the Holy Spirit), anointing and consignation whose performance was restricted to the episcopate.[2] In the non-Roman West, however, the liturgical history probably ran otherwise.[3] Some churches in Gaul apparently lacked an episcopal hand-laying and chrismation in the period directly before the Carolingian reform, knowing no hand-laying and only a single post-baptismal anointing (with which the gift of the Spirit was associated) which could be performed by presbyters. The same seems to have been true of Ireland before Roman influence from England caused the addition of the specifically episcopal acts in the twelfth century. The Spanish practice before the eleventh century (reflected in the *Liber Ordinum*, ed. M. Férotin, Paris, 1904) apparently was to allow the single chrismation and the hand-laying to the presbyterate, though an attempt was made in the seventh century to impose closer conformity with the Roman by restricting these two acts to the episcopate.

With this liturgical history the *theological* history[4] of the post-baptismal rites is interwoven. The major developments concerning the *meaning* of the post-baptismal rites are so important for the doctrine of what became the independent rite of confirmation that it is more convenient to delay describing them until we outline the modern Roman Catholic debate on the theology of that sacrament. But mention may be made here of the history of the *pastoral discipline* concerning the post-baptismal rites, for it was largely this that led to the recognition of "confirmation" as an independent sacrament which demanded a more careful theological rationale than had been necessary for the post-baptismal rites as long as they formed part of a complex of initiation that was regarded as a single whole.

The Western history of the pastoral discipline depends on the fact that, though presbyters were everywhere allowed to baptize, there was a restriction, from early days in Rome and eventually in the whole West, of certain post-baptismal acts to the episcopate.[5] This meant that, as the Church grew in numbers, presbyters celebrated baptisms away from the episcopal see, and the post-baptismal acts (apart from that first anointing immediately after the water which Rome allowed to the presbyter) had to wait for the visit of the bishop.[6] The time interval clearly emphasized the distinction between the baptism and the episcopal ceremonies but was not intended to destroy the fundamental unity of the initiation complex. It became usual in rural areas for several years to elapse between baptism and the episcopal acts, and parents came to have a low view of these latter and neglect to bring their children to the bishop. True, for candidates close enough to the episcopal see initiation was still for centuries celebrated as a complex whole at Easter or Pentecost; but even this procedure broke down when the Church came to place such emphasis on the peril of dying without baptism that presbyteral baptism within a few days of birth became the usual practice everywhere, so that even for infants living in the bishop's town the episcopal ceremonies became separated from baptism.

The practical fact of this gap of (in many cases) several years between baptism and the episcopal acts played a large part in bringing the scholastic theologians to recognize these last as the independent sacrament of confirmation with its own theology, and it became (to boot) a sacrament of which infants were not reckoned fit subjects. The Catechism of the Council of Trent only set the seal on the medieval development when it declared that the administration of confirmation was inexpedient before children had attained the use of reason.

The severance of communion from baptism did not proceed exactly apace with the above development. Without waiting until the bishop had performed the part which was peculiarly his according to the spreading Roman pattern of initiation, presbyters gave communion directly after baptism to the infants they baptized in the bishop's absence. In the twelfth century, however, the scrupulous respect for the eucharistic elements which accompanied the growth of an increasingly realistic understanding of Christ's presence in them led priests in some places to give to infants (who were for convenience communicated *sub specie sanguinis* only) unconsecrated wine, lest misfortune should befall the consecrated element itself; when, in the thirteenth century, it became more and more common for the eucharistic chalice to be withheld from the laity in general, the decline of the practice of communicating baptized infants was accelerated; by the end of the Middle Ages the practice had almost died out altogether and first communion had become securely associated with "the years of discretion".

All the Churches that stand heir to these Western developments have in recent years experienced questionings about their theology and practice of initiation. The most prominent of the theological problems has been that of the relation between baptism and confirmation. The debate in the Church of England at the end of the last century, in which A. T. Wirgman and Darwell Stone opposed the views of F. W. Puller and A. J. Mason, was resumed in the controversy centring on G. Dix and G. W. H. Lampe.[7]

Dix took up the arguments of Puller and Mason and claimed that according to Scripture and early tradition "confirmation" is the baptism of the Spirit "which 'seals' a man to eternity and for which baptism in water is only a preliminary". Western doctrine, however, has suffered a perversion, of which the introduction of the very word *con-*

firmatio instead of the older *consignatio* is an instance: "A document which needs 'sealing' is not valid until the seal has been affixed. The 'confirmation' of a document, though it may add to its authority, implies that it was already operative before it was 'confirmed'." The West has turned "confirmation" into a mere increase of a gift already imparted in baptism.

Lampe countered by maintaining that according to Scripture and earliest tradition the "seal", which is the gift of the indwelling Spirit, is normally given in water baptism.[8] Confirmation is not a "sacrament of the Gospel":[9] it may be reckoned as a rite which usefully allows a profession of faith by a person baptized in infancy, marks a significant moment in the baptized's subjective realization of the gifts already received in baptism,[10] makes clear his association with the apostolic task of the Church and, being episcopally administered, illustrates his link with the universal Church.

Several Roman Catholic scholars have been willing to come to the aid of the Anglicans in their difficulties. J. Ysebaert[11] has suggested that Anglicans have allowed themselves to be impaled on the horns of a false dilemma through talking about "the gift of the indwelling Spirit". He holds that there is in fact a distinction between the "indwelling of the Spirit" and the "gift of the Spirit",[12] and that the former begins with baptism while the latter is conferred in a post-baptismal rite.[13] Ysebaert can, however, establish this distinction and its ritual embodiment only at the cost of some strained exegesis of the New Testament texts and a refusal to allow in many cases for a fluidity in patristic terminology which he himself demonstrates to be present at least in some few cases.

Rather than accept Ysebaert's brave attempt to make the difficulty simply disappear, it is better to recognize frankly that there is in the Fathers, if not in the New Testament itself, some variety as to the moment of the "gift of the indwelling Spirit" in the total baptismal rite. While the liturgy kept baptism and the post-baptismal ceremonies together in a single rite, this variety, or even inconsistency,[14] did not make itself felt as a problem: this ancient variety itself may indeed permit a solution to the problem of the moment of the Spirit's bestowal which arose through the separation from baptism of the post-baptismal ceremonies to form the distinct rite of confirmation.

Thus Fr B. Leeming, for instance, has suggested[15] that the Anglican controversy is bedevilled by a failure to recognize that the "seal" and the "gift of the Spirit" may neither of them be single; and it is possible, as a result of the above-mentioned variety, to adduce patristic support for each part of Leeming's own contention that there is a gift of the Spirit and a seal at baptism, and a gift of the Spirit and a seal at confirmation. One is then left to distinguish between the two gifts and between the two seals. Leeming himself equates "seal" with what was later called "character" and argues that the confirmational character is a modification or enhancement[16] of the baptismal character.[17] In support of his case for a double *gift* of the Spirit, Leeming points out that the patristic writers associate the remission of sins and regeneration with the water (and this means, despite the Mason-Puller school, a gift of the Spirit Himself, since sanctifying grace involves, according to Scripture and tradition, the indwelling of the Holy Spirit, and not simply an action on the person from without), while the reception of the gifts of the Spirit connected with bearing witness to the faith is associated by the Fathers solely with the rites after baptism.

Leeming's solution to the Anglican controversy may suggest the right approach to the Roman Catholics' own problem on the meaning of confirmation, as we shall see presently; but it seems unlikely, despite its welcome emphasis on the gift of the Spirit at water baptism, to satisfy those who hold the classical doctrines of the Prayer Book and Articles, because it depends so much on the notion that the baptized person needs to be "perfected" sacramentally in confirmation. The difficulty is not so much that there may be multiple givings of the same Spirit, with varied and special ends in view: it is rather that something so basic to the Christian as his commission to, and equipment for, witness to Christ should be supposed ungiven in the primary act of baptism, and given only in the distinct sacrament of confirmation.[18]

The Roman Catholic Church has witnessed in the last generation an intensive inquiry[19] into its own understanding of confirmation. For long the emphasis of catechisms and dogmatic manuals has fallen on the idea of confirmation as the individual's "strengthening for the fight" in his personal battle against sin, and this understanding has been epitomized in the popular misinterpretation of the tap with which the bishop strikes the candidate's cheek as a symbol of combat rather than as a form of the kiss of peace. The notion of strengthening for the fight owes its prominence to the great influence exercised on the medieval development of the theology of confirmation by a much-quoted Whitsun sermon from fifth-century Gaul (now frequently ascribed to Faustus of Riez), and particularly by a catchword isolated from its context in the sermon: "... in baptismo regeneramur ad vitam, post baptismum confirmamur ad pugnam. In baptismo abluimur, post baptismum roboramur ...".[20]

This whole development, however, has had an axe laid at its roots by L. Bouyer, an axe whetted on Dix's stone. Bouyer[21] argues that the sole authentic doctrine of confirmation is the one which sees it as the completing seal of the baptismal complex; without it water baptism is so imperfect that the person who is merely baptized is not qualified to participate in the eucharist.

In recent years, a middling view has been advanced, with slightly differing emphases, by a growing number of theologians.[22] The patristic evidence for confirmation as the completing seal is given due weight; but there is an unwillingness to abandon the notion of "strengthening for the fight" altogether, for the picture of the post-baptismal rites as "arming" the Christian is as old as Tertullian and Cyril of Jerusalem.[23] It is noted, however, that in the medieval West the notion of preparation for the fight is often put in close proximity with another idea, namely the equipping of the Christian for witnessing to the faith, which figured prominently in the development of the theology of confirmation through the frequent quotation of a phrase evolved by Rabanus Maurus (+856) from his master Alcuin as an interpretation of the episcopal hand-laying: "A summo sacerdote per impositionem manus Paracletus traditur illi (baptizato) Spiritus Sanctus, ut roboretur per Spiritum Sanctum ad praedicandum aliis idem donum quod ipse in baptismate consecutus est."[24] The association of the post-baptismal acts with the Christian's witness to the faith can be seen, so it is urged, in the connection which especially the Easterns[25] are fond of making between the aromatic oil of the chrismation and the Pauline image of Christians as the sweet savour of Christ in the world (2 Cor. 2: 14–17). Drawing attention to Christ's promise of the Holy Spirit for the disciples in their public witness to Himself (Matt. 10: 18–20 and par.) the mediating theologians argue that the strengthening in confirmation should be interpreted as referring, not so narrowly to the confirmed's private battle against sin, but more to his brave and faithful witness to his Lord before the world (of which witness his own holiness of life, of course, forms part). They see the "completion" bestowed in confirmation, therefore, as above all the gift of the Holy Spirit for the purpose of sharing in the apostolate of the Church. The Spirit has already been imparted in baptism, but now He comes again for a purpose which is characteristically His, namely the furtherance of the Mission.[26]

An outsider may perhaps be forgiven both for pointing out that this stress on the apostolate finds little support in the Roman liturgy of confirmation actually in use and also for remarking on the oddness of the fact that the rite does not call on the confirmed to make profession of the faith which he is being commissioned and equipped to preach to others.[27]

The Reformed (Presbyterian) Churches, especially on the continent of Europe, have also been busy seeking an understanding of their own confirmation.[28] Bold suggestions have come from Max Thurian, sub-prior of the Taizé Community, and from Professor J.-J. von Allmen of Neuchâtel.

Thurian has advocated a baptismal rite which would include in a unified whole the two moments of water baptism and Spirit baptism (expressed in hand-laying); this would usually be administered to infants. Confirmation would be administered when the baptized person freely decided to commit himself to service within the Church: it would confer a renewal of the Holy Spirit who would give the gifts necessary for such service.[29] But von Allmen[30] objects that Thurian's understanding of confirmation as the ordination of all the willing baptized "to the service of the Church", with no particular ministry specified, is a perpetuation of the opinion, common in the Reformed tradition but unacceptable because it allows confirmation to detract from baptism, that it is only at confirmation that one is admitted to the full rights and duties of Church membership.

Von Allmen's own fundamental contention is that it is wrong to tackle the problem of confirmation from the assumption that confirmation is a fixed datum of ecclesiastical practice which only needs to be interpreted: "confirmation" as an independent rite is rather a fact of ecclesiastical tradition which must be subjected to the judgment of Scripture, and a solution to its problem will come only when *baptismal* theology and practice have regained their New Testament fullness. New Testament "baptism" comprises three moments: baptism of water (=judgment on the present age), baptism of Spirit (=the baptized's rebirth to the age to come), and confession of faith. It is von Allmen's plea that the Reformed Churches should re-introduce immersion in place of their current practice of aspersion, should introduce an imposition of hands with prayer for the Spirit, and should demand, not merely an undertaking by the parents that they will bring up the child in the Christian faith, but "vicarious vows" taken by sponsors for the infant.

Such a full rite of baptism would leave no room for confirmation to be understood, in a way derogatory to baptism itself, as the baptism of the Spirit[31] or as the *first* profession of faith.[32] If confirmation were to be retained at all, it would be as the first *renewal* of baptismal vows undertaken, after a post-baptismal catechumenate, in the context of an annual Paschal renewal by the whole congregation.

It may be thought, however, that, as a solution to the problem of faith in the baptism of infants, von Allmen's suggestion of vicarious vows and confession involves difficulties at least as great as those in the position, dismissed by von Allmen as Pietist, that the baptism of infants remains on man's side incomplete until a *first* profession of faith at a later date.

Lutheranism is also experiencing a crisis in its understanding of confirmation, particularly in Germany. A guide to the Lutheran debate can be found in the study document prepared by Dr Joachim Heubach for the Fourth Assembly of the Lutheran World Federation, Helsinki 1963.[33] Heubach summarizes the deliberations of two conferences held under the auspices of the L.W.F. Commission on Education: the first had been arranged by the German Churches at Hofgeismar in 1958,[34] the second had been an international seminar held at Loccum in 1961.[35] Two understandings of confirmation are rejected out of hand: confirmation does not confer "full membership" or "adult membership", and where such phrases have crept into Lutheran rites from the Free Churches they must be eliminated, since they run counter to the Lutheran view that full membership is given in baptism; equally to be removed are the eighteenth and nineteenth century accretions which associate confirmation with a bestowal of certain *legal* privileges in the Church.

Care must be taken at certain other points also. The candidates should not be asked to take vows for a future over which they have no control (their place in the rite dates from Pietist and Rationalist days), but neither (in reaction against such vows, or out of a desire to avoid the view, Pietist also, of confirmation as a *completion* of the baptismal covenant by a subjective confession of faith) should the confession of faith be removed altogether. What is needed is a confession of faith suitable to the understanding of confirmation as an "intensive" form of the *anamnesis* of baptism which should take place in daily repentance and obedience throughout the Christian life.

The idea of baptismal *anamnesis* should also govern the hand-laying with prayer which takes place in confirmation. Confirmation is a remembrance, in the Spirit, of the gifts already given in baptism which are the foundation of daily Christian living, and this reference back to baptism is needed to hold in check the tendency in some Lutheran groups to place such a lop-sided emphasis on the laying on of hands accompanied by words of blessing that confirmation threatens to become an independent sacrament.[36]

The positive contention of the L.W.F. study document is this. The rite of confirmation is properly a special moment within the total post-baptismal catechumenate which lasts throughout the Christian life; it is the liturgical conclusion of the "children's catechumenate" and marks the transition to the more advanced forms of the youth and adult catechumenates; it is a particularly intensive occasion of baptismal *anamnesis* in a Christian life in which the gifts and obligations conferred in baptism are being constantly recalled. It remains to be seen how far the L.W.F. document will influence the theology and practice of confirmation in the Lutheran Churches.

In both Congregationalism and Methodism, the primary problem of initiation is to understand what is meant by "membership of the Church". Is membership conferred in baptism which is most usually administered in infancy? Or is it conferred at a later date in a service which is called by Congregationalists "The Reception of Church Members on Profession of Faith"[37] and by Methodists "The Public Reception of New Members"?[38] At the baptism of an infant, both Congregationalists and Methodists declare that they "receive this child into the congregation of Christ's flock", while at the later service, in which the person is called on to confess faith in Christ, each begins by talking of an impending reception "into full communion with the Church", the Methodist minister saying subsequently, "We now welcome you into the fellowship of Christ's Church", and the Congregationalist, "We receive and welcome you to membership of the Church, to share in all its privileges and responsibilities."

The charge may be laid against Methodists and Congregationalists that they detract from baptism by using the word "membership" only in connection with the service which is observed years later. But may not these two Free Churches demand serious consideration for the contention implicit in their initiation liturgies that, even though a person has been received into Christ's flock as an infant, something *new* happens when the Christian comes to confess his Lord *with his own lips*?

It may be unfortunate that "membership of the Church" is not associated *expressis verbis* with the baptism of an infant (though reception "into Christ's flock" comes very close), but it seems at least an arguable possibility that upon confession of faith a person already baptized as an infant becomes *a different kind of member* of the Church, with no doubts cast on the fact that he was already within the Church.

The statement of the Methodist Conference on *Church Membership* (London, 1961) may not be far astray when it speaks of "two kinds of membership", the first being conferred by infant baptism, the second beginning with a service of "entry into the *committed* membership of Christ's Church".

In any church in which baptism is administered before an age of personal confession of faith, it seems to me impossible that "Church membership" should be an internally undifferentiated category in substance or in practice, however rigorously (say) the Lutheran may restrict the *terminology* of Church membership to baptism and however carelessly the Methodist or the Congregationalist may associate the *word* "membership" *tout court* with the service in which one makes personal profession of faith.

Apart from the question of the relation between baptism and "confirmation" another complex of problems, in which doctrinal and practical strands are intertwined, has resulted from the medieval development in the West. At what age should confirmation be administered? At what age should communion first be given? What is the relation, if any, between confirmation and first communion?

In the Roman Catholic Church confirmation and communion are usually reserved for "the age of reason" or "the years of discretion". Confirmation is not a prerequisite for communion, baptism sufficing;[39] and communion is given as soon as the child is considered old enough to prepare for it by sacramental confession, that is from the age of about six or seven. The age of confirmation varies in practice, and arguments of a more or less theological nature are brought in favour of the different possibilities.

The French episcopate has indicated[40] that confirmation should be given about the age of seven, and French writers support this by reference to the child's need for strengthening in his faith and witness, especially when his everyday environment, and even perhaps his own family, is to a great degree dechristianized. Some English Catholics advocate confirmation at eleven or twelve, so that the sacrament would coincide with the important transition from primary to secondary school.

In German-speaking countries some pastoral theologians have argued for confirmation at the age of going out from school to confront the adult world. The French theologians tend to criticize such attempts to "postpone" confirmation either as smacking of a "sacrament of puberty" (after a pagan pattern) or as depending on a misunderstanding of Thomas Aquinas's connection of confirmation with "spiritual maturity" in a way which places spiritual development in too close a parallel with physical and psychological development.

But it seems a fair retort that, granting the rightness of infant baptism and of early communion (itself a repeated renewal of the benefits of baptism), there is much advantage in the use of confirmation, which in any case is far from having a consistent history in either theology or practice, as marking an important stage in a person's total human life. It may very well be argued that there is a close relationship between physical, psychological and social development on the one hand and at least *possible* "spiritual" development on the other, admitting of course that many people who are otherwise adult suffer from arrested spiritual development, and that children may possess a faith which is perfect or mature *within the limits imposed by their age* though not so rich as that possible to adults.[41]

In the Lutheran, Reformed, and Anglican traditions, admission to communion is associated with confirmation. On the continent of Europe, Protestant confirmation and first communion usually take place at about fifteen, with a whole age group being confirmed *en masse*; but, in order to counteract the widespread tendency for this first communion also to be *last* communion, there are proposals in various quarters that first communion at least should be administered earlier, at (say) ten or twelve, each child's case being considered individually by pastor and parents. This early first communion would be preceded by basic catechetical instruction. Confirmation might also be moved forward to this occasion of first communion,[42] or else it might be kept for a later date, when it would mark the conclusion of a catechumenate to the level of that with which the present confirmation is already associated[43] or would signal the Christian's ordination to service in the Church.[44]

In the Church of England Prayer Books, catechism (comprising instruction in the Apostles' Creed, the Ten Commandments, the Lord's Prayer and the meaning of baptism and of the Lord's Supper) and confirmation have always been intimately linked; and a rubric at the end of the order of confirmation states that "there shall none be admitted to the holy Communion, until such time as he be confirmed, or be ready and desirous to be confirmed". In some areas of "high church" persuasion, confirmation and first communion may be administered as early as seven, while "evangelical" practice tends to place them about the age of fourteen.

It is striking that, whatever variety there may exist in the understanding of "confirmation" within and among these three traditions (Lutheran, Reformed, Anglican) stemming from the classical Reformation, there is general agreement that communion should be given only when one is of an age to profess faith, and that after due instruction.[45] And again one is still left wondering on what grounds it is that communion is withheld through the early years of childhood from persons who have been baptized as infants and who have committed no breach of ecclesiastical discipline.[46]

We started this chapter with the intention of seeking *advantages* in the Western practice of delaying "confirmation" (however understood) and communion in the case of persons baptized in infancy, granted the rightness of infant baptism. But it is, in fact, in terms of *problems* that we have found ourselves discussing the various situations that obtain in the Churches which stand heir to the developments in the medieval West. Baptism is administered in infancy, but there remain for enactment in subsequent years some or all of a series of events (catechumenate,[47] personal profession of faith, post-baptismal acts, and first communion) which in origin were included in a totality of which *baptism itself was the key*. Is it, then, surprising that there should be problems involved both in relating each of these other events to the key of baptism from which they are now isolated and also in relating them among themselves? Weaknesses may be found in every attempted solution which allows the pattern to remain fragmented.

May it be that there is no satisfactory answer to the Western problems apart from the restoration of a unified initiatory complex of which baptism is the key? The choice would be between (1) bringing the other events into infancy to join baptism and (2) postponing baptism until it could once more hold the other events together in a whole. The difficulties involved in the former course were apparent in the discussion on the Eastern Churches: the advantages of keeping some of the events of the baptismal complex, and particularly the catechumenate[48] and the profession of faith, for an age of reason are equally manifest.

Is it then possible to "grant the rightness of infant baptism"? Would it be a better choice to abandon the baptism of infants? Even within Western Churches practising infant baptism there have been recent advocates of this course, sometimes arguing on absolute theological grounds,[49] more frequently making out a practical case on the basis of the historical situation in which their churches find themselves today. Of this latter type of case more will be said in chapter VI.

Before that we look at the Churches of the Baptist movement which have, of deliberate theological principle, for centuries rejected the practice of infant baptism: we examine the case they present, both historical and theological, against the baptism of infants and in favour of the baptism solely of professing believers.

IV

BELIEVERS' BAPTISM

THE ONLY persons unambiguously recorded by the New Testament as having received baptism were adults: the earliest undisputed evidence for the baptism of infants is Tertullian's dissuasive against the practice in his book *On Baptism* (chapter 18) written in the opening years of the third century. True, Origen (*circa* 185–254) believed that "the Church has received a tradition from the apostles to give baptism even to little children (*parvulis*)";[1] but modern theologians are probably more exacting than Origen in their demands for historical proof of the baptism of infants from New Testament times. The evidence adduced in recent studies falls under three heads: (1) Analogies with Jewish practice; (2) Inferences from New Testament texts; (3) Other literary witnesses.

1. As the sign of entry into the New Covenant, Christian baptism corresponds to circumcision, the ceremony of initiation into the Old Covenant. Cyprian[2] recognizes the validity of this analogy even when he recommends the baptism of infants without waiting for the eighth day after birth, which was the day when Jewish male children were circumcised; and it is possible that the analogy influenced Christian baptism from the start.

The children of Jewish proselytes were both circumcised (if male) and baptized at their parents' entry into Judaism. If Jewish proselyte baptism influenced Christian baptism (and it is now the general trend of scholarly opinion that proselyte baptism was at least practised by the time of Jesus), then it is conceivable that Christian baptism also was administered to infants from the beginning.

2. Much is made of the ancient solidarity of the family in discussion of the New Testament references to the baptism of households;[3] the Old Testament suggests that not only a man's slaves but his children belong to his household, and these too would be included in the baptism which followed the father's conversion. Children appear to be addressed as members of the Church in the Letters to the Colossians (3: 20) and Ephesians (6: 1), both letters being meant for "the saints"

according to their opening sentences. Cullmann[4] has suggested that κωλύειν was a technical term from early baptismal liturgy (cf. Acts 8: 36; 10: 47; 11: 17): its use in the incident of Jesus's blessing of the children is due to an attempt to settle an early controversy on the baptism of children by appeal to a dominical command to "forbid them not". The Church of Scotland's Special Commission on Baptism[5] points out that men, women *and children* were included in the Mosaic Exodus, which is proposed as a type of Christian baptism in 1 Cor. 10: 1ff.

3. Justin Martyr describes as living in his own day "many men and women who were discipled to Christ from their childhood (*οἱ ἐκ παίδων ἐμαθητεύθησαν τῷ Χριστῷ*)".[6] On the point of his martyrdom around the middle of the second century, Polycarp's proud claim was, "Eighty-six years I have been His slave";[7] which might suggest that he had been baptized very young, and that by about the year 65. This kind of evidence would admittedly be valuable only as support to an already strong case.

None of this alleged evidence has been left undisputed, even by scholars who cannot be suspected of having any doctrinaire Baptist axe to grind. The Lutheran, K. Aland, for example, has raised formidable objections to Jeremias's[8] interpretations of historical evidence, even though he himself maintains the rightness of infant baptism on theological grounds. But Baptist scholars have excelled in demonstrating the weaknesses in the historical case for a primitive practice of infant baptism. H. H. Rowley[9] has shown that the appeal to the analogy of Jewish proselyte baptism is a two-edged sword; for children born to proselytes subsequently to their parents' conversion were not baptized, but only circumcised; paedobaptists who use the analogy for the sake of the baptism of converts' children already born must therefore be prepared to admit that the Jewish practice also tells *against* the baptism of infants born after the parents have become Christian.

Nor can the analogy of circumcision be unquestioningly applied to Christian baptism in every detail, even though both are rites of initiation. Contrary to those who believe that the elements of similarity and continuity are more important than the element of antithesis in the relation between baptism and circumcision envisaged in Col. 2: 11–12, G. R. Beasley-Murray[10] holds that no case can be built on those verses for an identity in the conditions of administering Christian baptism and the Jewish rite of circumcision since Christian baptism is there regarded as mediating the "circumcision of the heart" for which the prophets had hoped (e.g. Deut. 30: 6; cf. Rom. 2: 28f., Phil. 3: 3) rather than as fulfilling the *external rite* of circumcision which did not possess that spiritual meaning. In that passage, moreover, Paul stresses the place of faith in the operation of baptism; if the Church was encouraged by Jewish circumcision to baptize the infant children of Christian parents, then its practice was not in accord with Paul's theology of baptism. The most that can be said is that Christian baptism resembles its Jewish antecedents in some points.[11] Since there is no *exact* correspondence between the Jewish and the Christian rites, the bearing of the former on the Christian baptism of infants is open to dispute.

Inferences from the New Testament in favour of a primitive practice of infant baptism are also open to criticism. "Household" may mean slaves and not children. Moreover, the accounts of the baptism of the households of the Philippian jailer and of Crispus stress the place of belief in baptism (Acts 16: 31–34; 18: 8). The children addressed in Col. 3: 20 and Eph. 6: 1 were obviously of an age to understand the apostle's exhortations and may therefore have been baptized on confession of faith. Cullmann's *κωλύειν* has received a hammering from Markus Barth:[12] The three questions in which the verb occurs in Acts give no ground for believing that there was ever a *real* question regularly repeated in the baptismal liturgy like: "Is there anything to prevent such and such a person from being baptized?"; the point of the "questions" in Acts (those in 10:47 and 11: 17 at least are rhetorical) is precisely to show that nothing or no one may hinder the baptism of a person who asks for it or to whom God has given the Spirit; Acts 11: 17 would indeed involve the strange picture of God standing before Peter the *Kirchenfürst* and begging permission for the Gentiles to be baptized. It would be unwise to see in 1 Cor. 10: 1ff. a correspondence between type and antitype in every point: the passage is a subsidiary introduction to an ethical exhortation, not a dogmatic statement on the sacraments.

We know that infant baptism was practised at least from the turn of the second and third centuries; but this period also marked the heyday of adult baptism. For many converts came to the Church even during the years of persecution; and the imperial recognition of Christianity begun by Constantine brought people to baptism in their droves. By the fifth or sixth century, the Roman Empire had few adults remaining to be converted, and infant baptism was left as the preponderant practice of the Church. But as late as the fourth century, when infant baptism had long been a usual practice, several famous sons with at least one Christian parent were not baptized until they had reached manhood: Gregory of Nazianzus, Basil, Jerome, Rufinus, Paulinus of Nola, Augustine. Other people, like the Emperor Constantine himself (+337), deferred baptism until the latest possible moment before death on account of the gravity of post-baptismal sin;[13] but the would-be *clinici* (from κλίνη: bed, sick-bed) who sought to leave this life with their newly acquired baptismal innocence intact provoked attack from preachers [14] who clearly saw such tarrying as an unwillingness to assume the moral responsibilities which would be imposed for life by a baptism in earlier years.

Certainly the classical liturgies of baptism took shape in a period when adult initiation (and not merely on the deathbed) was a usual practice. They provide both for a catechumenate in which instruction and ceremonies go hand in hand and also for certain conscious actions, like the renunciation of Satan and the profession of faith, on the part of the candidates at the time of baptism. These liturgies continued in use, with little or no adaptation, even when infant baptism became the wellnigh exclusive practice, though parts of them which were appropriate enough for adults would never have been introduced into a liturgy specially designed for infant initiation.

Apart from the baptism of newly converted nations (sometimes brought simultaneously into the Church as into the Empire at the point of the sword), the medieval Church knew almost exclusively infant baptism, with both "confirmation" and first communion becoming divorced from it in the West, as we have seen in chapter III. There were a few experiments at believers' baptism, like that of the Adoptionist Paulicians in Armenia at the beginning of the ninth century[15] and that of the Petrobrusians around Toulouse at the start of the twelfth century. But it was not until the Reformation that the baptism solely of professing believers was proclaimed and practised with theological vigour on a wide scale. The Lutheran and Reformed traditions retained infant baptism, despite the difficulties which the original Reformers found in accommodating the practice to their principle of justification by faith alone. But, beginning from Zürich, Anabaptism[16] spread through much of Europe, often driven on by persecution, and sometimes totally suppressed. The Dutchman, Menno Simons, assembled the Anabaptist remnants of northern Europe into a movement which still bears his name—the Mennonites. It was on the soil of Holland that separatist refugees from England formed the first English Baptist church in 1609, the forerunner of the great Anglo-Saxon Baptist communion. A group from this church, led by Thomas Helwys, returned to London to found the first known Baptist Church in England, at Spitalfields in 1612. Such were the beginnings of the movement which at its best stands for the view of the visible Church as a separated congregation of professed believers who live according to the moral responsibilities laid upon them in their adult baptism.

Controversy (if the word is not too mild) there has certainly been from the very beginnings of the Baptist movement, but Baptists took stangely little part in the early stages of the modern ecumenical debate on baptism. To be sure, the Baptist representatives felt impelled to add a footnote to the main statement on baptism produced by the second World Conference on Faith and Order held in Edinburgh in 1937, making clear that it was only to those "capable of making a personal confession of faith" that they could apply the sentence, "Baptism is a gift of God's redeeming love to the Church; and, administered with water in the name of the Father, the Son, and the Holy Spirit, is a sign and seal of Christian discipleship in obedience to our Lord's command." But the stand taken by Baptists and the Disciples of Christ[17] was often regarded simply as their particular denominational idiosyncrasy. That baptism moved from the periphery of the ecumenical scene to a position near its centre was due in no small measure to the work of the two theologians, Brunner and Barth.

In *Wahrheit als Begegnung* (1938)[18] Emil Brunner argued that "baptism is not only an act of grace, but just as much an act of confession stemming from the act of grace". Not satisfied by Lutheran or Reformed attempts to relate the New Testament theology to infant baptism, he characterized contemporary practice as "hardly anything short of scandalous".

First delivered as a lecture to Swiss theological students in May 1943, Karl Barth's *Die kirchliche Lehre von der Taufe* contains a powerful appeal for the abandonment of infant baptism in favour of believers' baptism, but with no re-baptism meanwhile, as he bids be noted by "Anabaptists of all kinds—Roman and those supposed to be evangelical". It is Jesus Christ, working through the Church, who is "the primary and true Baptizer", but the candidate for baptism is certainly "the second most important figure" in the drama. Through baptism, Jesus Christ speaks and acts (it is Barth's massive assertion) with a *cognitive* purpose (and not causative or generative, as Romans, Lutherans and Anglicans maintain), assuring the believer that salvation is already his and telling him that he is now pledged to the obedient service of his Lord for the glorifying of God in the upbuilding of the Church. The nature, power and meaning of baptism are dependent on its divine origin, and therefore no baptism can be rendered null by any inadequacy in the human ordering and practice of baptism on the part either of the Church which administers or of the person who receives the sacrament. But this does not absolve the baptizing Church from effort to regain that unity and that one pure faith in the absence of which the content of baptism, though objectively present, is obscured to the understanding. Nor does it mean that the baptism of infants is any other than a disorder when the proper order, according to New Testament exegesis and the nature of the thing, requires "the responsible willingness and readiness of the baptized person to receive the promise of grace directed towards him and to be party to the pledge of allegiance concerning the grateful service demanded of him".

In Switzerland, the matter was pursued in the books by F. J. Leenhardt, O. Cullmann and M. Barth mentioned in chapter I. Then there has been the fierce controversy between J. Jeremias and K. Aland about the historical evidence for a primitive practice of infant baptism (see p. 96, n. 8). Baptists began to play a significant part in the debate with the publication of works by Johannes Schneider[19] in Germany and Neville Clark in Britain.

In *An Approach to the Theology of the Sacraments* (London, 1956), Clark argues that a detailed biblical, historical and theological investigation into baptism, necessary as it is in the current controversy, risks distortion if it is conducted in isolation. Any attempt to reach a satisfactory theology of baptism should be carried out only in conjunction with a reconsideration of eucharistic doctrine, with both sacraments firmly set within the total context of Christology, ecclesiology and eschatology. For baptism and eucharist together are grounded in the atoning work of Christ. Baptism is the sacrament of the individual's initiation into the community of the Church which at every eucharist is remade—as it offers itself in union with its Lord and receives His sacramental body—into that broken and glorified body of Christ which it mystically is. The eucharist is the representative anticipation of that final transfiguration of the whole creation which was included in the scope of the redemption wrought once at Calvary and then become effective for every Christian in his baptism.

One of the most thorough Baptist contributions to the ecumenical debate is the symposium entitled *Christian Baptism*,[20] the work of ten ministers, each having submitted his paper to discussion by the whole group. The biblical scholars spend much energy in demolishing alleged New Testament evidences for the apostolic practice of infant baptism. Already Tertullian[21] had denied that the saying of Jesus "Forbid them not" warranted the baptizing of children before they were of an age to recognize Him to whom they come. R. E. O. White attacks the apologetic use of such incidents as the Lord's blessing of the children (made, for instance, by the Church of Scotland's Commission on Baptism) with a vehemence which matches Tertullian's in full rhetorical flow. Inferences of the baptism of infants from phrases in Acts and in the Epistles are also sharply criticized.

But even if (as Baptists hold) there is no biblical evidence that baptism was administered to infants in apostolic times, the matter of the rightness of later and modern practice is still not settled, as S. F. Winward shows in an irenic chapter under the title "Scripture, Tradition, and Baptism".

Winward starts with the opening "declaration of principle" of the Baptist Union of Great Britain and Ireland "that our Lord and Saviour Jesus Christ, God manifest in the flesh, is the sole and absolute authority in all matters pertaining to faith and practice, as revealed in the Holy Scriptures, and that each church has liberty, under the guidance of the Holy Spirit, to interpret and administer His laws".

He argues that this statement does not do justice to the Tradition of the total Church down the centuries as a medium of authority. For primitive material was transmitted not only in the Scriptures but also in the worship, teaching and ethical practice of the ongoing life of the Church. Moreover, the Lord Himself continues to live in His Church, and the Holy Spirit takes the things of Christ and declares them to the Church. So far the way would be open to the practice of baptizing infants, even though it be a "scriptureless thing".[22] But this "positive and appreciative attitude" to ecclesiastical Tradition, Winward declares, must not be uncritical: the total Tradition must always be judged by the canon of that part of the Tradition deposited in written form in the New Testament Scriptures, since these are the indubitable work of those closest to the central events of the salvation accomplished through Jesus Christ. Even within the New Testament it is proper to distinguish between what is temporary (e.g. 1 Cor. 11: 2–6) and what is permanent (e.g. 1 Cor. 11: 17–34); here the yardstick is, "*essential* practice arises out of the very nature of the Gospel itself".

As to baptism, the question now runs: Is the New Testament practice of believers' baptism a temporary phenomenon arising out of the "special missionary situation" of the Church? Or does believers' baptism rather enshrine an essential truth of the Gospel which is belied by the administration of baptism to infants?

The Baptist cannot now simply say: infant baptism is not recorded in the New Testament, *therefore* it is wrong. Rather he must show that the baptism only of believers arises out of the Gospel itself.

The more important part of the work of the New Testament scholars in the symposium, *Christian Baptism*, is therefore their attempt to demonstrate that repentance, faith and ethical responsibility are essential concomitants of baptism according to the New Testament Gospel. When Peter had proclaimed at Pentecost the redemption accomplished through Jesus Christ, he called upon his audience, "Repent and be baptized . . ." (Acts 2: 38). Baptism is frequently linked with "hearing the Gospel" or "believing" (Acts 2: 41; 8: 12; 8: 37, Western text; 16: 14f.; 16: 31–34; 18: 8; 19: 5; cf. Rom. 10: 8–10, a passage which scholars are practically unanimous in associating with a primitive baptismal creed). It is through *faith* in the operation of God who raised Christ from the dead that Christians, in the baptism in which they shared Christ's burial, have also been raised to life together with Christ (Col. 2: 11–13). This baptism, in which Christians have appropriated the death and resurrection of Christ, is the basis for ethical exhortation: Christians are called upon to live out the practical implications of this being henceforth dead to sin and alive to God in Christ Jesus (Rom. 6; cf. Gal. 3: 27; and Col. 3: 1–14 and 1 Cor 6: 8–11, which both bear the unmistakable stamp of baptism).

Evidence such as this had already led the Methodist, W. F. Flemington,[23] to conclude that the typical New Testament baptism was that of an adult believer and that the New Testament theology of baptism cannot be applied to the baptism of infants *without modification*. But can there in fact be one theology for the baptism of adults and another theology for the baptism of infants, without implying that there are really two distinct sacraments, adult baptism and infant baptism, rather than the one sacrament of baptism sometimes administered to believers, sometimes to infants?

If the full-bodied New Testament theology of baptism cannot be applied to the baptism administered to infants, then perhaps Baptists are right to call for the abandonment of the practice of baptizing infants. Baptists can fairly point out that according to the clearest New Testament scheme repentance and faith preceded baptism, and baptism had its own immediate ethical consequences; nor would any upholder of infant baptism deny that repentance, faith and righteous living form the proper human response to God's grace. But one may at least ask whether the faith that is *decisively* related to baptism is not the faith which comes *after* baptism and must be continued throughout life (with inevitable implications for conduct) rather than the faith professed *before* baptism. (Profession of faith before baptism might be seen, with Cullmann, not as a human precondition for baptism but as a divine indication that baptism shall be administered, an indication which might be given in another way, as in the case in Acts 10: 44ff. and also perhaps in the case of the birth of children into a Christian family.)

The point at issue is whether, by altering the best attested New Testament sequence, the practice of administering baptism at a considerable interval in time apparently before even the beginnings of repentance and faith and the assumption of moral responsibility does such violence to the relation between divine initiative and human response in the work of salvation that such baptism ceases to be a true embodiment of the Gospel.

It is Neville Clark who digs deepest, when he tries to ground the theology of believers' baptism in the total pattern of the Christological economy of salvation. In the first place, baptism into Christ must mirror the rhythm of divine initiative and human response displayed in the incarnation and earthly work of Jesus Christ, the True Man who "although he was a Son learned obedience through what he suffered" (Heb. 5–8). The historical basis of the rite of Christian baptism is the Baptism of Christ in the Jordan and the fulfilment in cross, resurrection and ascension to which both the divine action and the human obedience in that Baptism pointed: "The primacy of the divine is clearly shown forth in the experience of Christ at Jordan; yet the obedient response of the True Man is here made crucial and explicit".[24] And second: Christian baptism belongs to the time of tension between the first coming of Christ and His final advent. The kingdom was actualized and established by the Cross; at the Parousia it will be perfected and acclaimed; meanwhile the Church is the place where the kingdom is already acknowledged, and baptism is the sign of the Church, the rite in which the kingdom is acknowledged and extended.

Baptism is not a declaratory sign that the whole world is marked for redemption (no such declaratory sign is needed, beyond the cross itself): baptism is rather the conscious appropriation of redemption and the conscious acknowledgment of God's kingdom; it is where man's

Amen is spoken, and *Christus pro nobis* becomes *Christus in nobis.*

For all his stress on the need for human action in baptism, Clark is careful to safeguard the necessity of the divine, and in this he avoids the trap which has caught many a Baptist: to emphasize baptism so strongly as the occasion of a public profession of faith (a simple declaration or ratification of what has happened on the human side in "conversion") that the God-to-man movement in it is lost and the rite ceases to be a sacrament.

There are indications, however, that Baptist thought is moving more and more towards a sacramental understanding of the baptismal rite. Clark's grounding of baptism in Christology provides the ultimate justification for this, since Christ is the prime sacrament of the encounter between God and man; from Him the Church and its sacraments must all take their origin.[25] Clark himself holds that baptism in the New Testament was an *effective* sign of God's grace: "Baptism, in this normative period, implies, embodies and effects forgiveness of sin, initiation into the church and the gift of the Holy Spirit."[26] The scriptural support for this view outcrops at several points in the work of the biblical scholars in *Christian Baptism,* e.g.

1. A. Gilmore regards the symbolic act of the Old Testament prophets as an antecedent of baptism. Though these acts may have had historical roots in mimetic magic, prophetic symbolism differs from magic in that it does not aim to change the will of God but rather proclaims the will of God and helps it to become effective. When Christian baptism is seen against this background, the way is open to an understanding of it as a declaratory and effective sign of God's purpose to bring the particular candidate to salvation.

2. S. I. Buse points out the differences in the moment of the Spirit's bestowal in the incidents recorded in Acts, but he is prepared to allow that Acts 2: 38 links baptism and the gift of the Spirit. Buse considers it significant, moreover, that Acts records no case of self-baptism: the convert was baptized by a person acting as the representative of the Lord.

3. G. R. Beasley-Murray shows that, according to Paul, baptism is not only man's act of confessing the faith but is also God's act of salvation (Rom. 10: 9–10). The activity of the believer in crucifying the flesh (Gal. 5: 24) or stripping off the old nature (Col. 3: 9)[27] is the counterpart of his receptivity and submission which are betokened by the aorist passives of Rom. 6. In baptism, the believer *is buried, is united* with the form of Christ's death, *is crucified* with Him; he receives

something which he cannot produce for himself. Beasley-Murray concludes from these and other Pauline texts that for Paul "baptism was . . . an effective sign; in it Christ and faith come together in the meeting of conversion".

When baptism is regarded in this sacramental way, then the *mode* of baptism becomes a question worthy of consideration. For if God has chosen to act through a symbolic action, the symbol should correspond to the purpose of the divine action. As the effective sign of a complete washing from sin and the mimetic appropriation of the death, burial and resurrection of Jesus Christ, baptism is aptly performed by total immersion.

Baptist scholarship will probably never know another F. W. Gotch, whose *A Critical Rendering of the Word βαπτίζω* (1841) studied the translations of the word in thirty-three languages, ancient and modern, in order to prove the necessity of dipping or plunging the whole body under water.[28] But Baptists are right to point to ancient evidence[29] in favour of total immersion and to the continuing practice of the Byzantine Churches. Affusion[30] or even sprinkling[31] may well suffice in circumstances of cold, illness, or shortage of water; but, in their insistence on total immersion as the *normative* practice, Baptists can teach a salutary lesson on the correspondence between sign and thing signified to some of the denominations which are ostensibly more sacramental in their theology of baptism.

These developments in Baptist thought have taken place among the scholars. Is there evidence that they have percolated to the man in the pew—and to his children sitting beside him? In the current Baptist Church Hymnal the emphasis falls on the action of the believer receiving baptism. But in a manual for ministers compiled by E. A. Payne and S. F. Winward under the title, *Orders and Prayers for Church Worship* (1960), there is a suggested service for the baptism of believers based on the following principle: "In the order for Believers' Baptism . . . it is not sufficient to set forth the response required of the candidates; a whole, balanced service must also declare the divine action and promises." According to the order of service, the benefits received from the Lord in the sacrament are death and resurrection with Christ, cleansing from sin, the gift of the Holy Spirit and membership of the Church; and for all "who profess repentance toward God and faith in our Lord Jesus Christ" baptism is a following of Christ's example and command, a "public confession of personal faith" in Him as Saviour and Lord and a "vow or pledge of allegiance" to Him.

Evaluation of Believers' Baptism

If it could be shown beyond doubt that the apostles baptized infants, then the upholders of infant baptism could ask Baptists to think twice before rejecting a practice begun by those who had been closest to the central events of the salvation accomplished through Christ—though even that rejection would be justified if, on account of changed circumstances, the practice were no longer a true embodiment of the Gospel. But since the historical question remains open (for it is no more proved that baptism was administered solely to professing believers than it is that infants also received baptism), it is in the courts of theology that the main debate must take place. Here the Baptist case is a strong one. And a man like Neville Clark is a worthy advocate. Rooted in the mystery of the person and work of Jesus Christ Himself, True God and True Man, Christian baptism is the effective enactment of an encounter between God and man in which the benefits of Christ's atoning work are conveyed to the penitent believer, bringing him into the Church in which the Kingdom is acknowledged. What are the theological arguments that can be marshalled against that?

1. A theologian must be on his guard against drawing too direct consequences on the pattern of divine initiative and human response from the case of Jesus Christ. For other men do not enjoy the same hypostatic union between divine and human natures which was Jesus Christ's. When there is less than perfect co-ordination between the two moments, then we need to be particularly clear that the priority lies with the divine, not with the human.

The Baptist position is a valuable pointer to the human response which is necessary for the appropriation of salvation; but the priority of grace may find a valuable safeguard in the baptism of infants. That God has *already* wrought the unique act of universal salvation through Jesus Christ is clear, and infant baptism is not needed to keep plain the priority of *that* act of grace; to make baptism into a simple *declaratory* sign of the general salvation already enacted is a reduction of the sacrament against which Baptists are right to issue a warning. No, baptism is *the actual application of salvation to an individual*, and it is in this precise case of individual salvation that baptismal practice must not appear to jeopardize the priority of God.

It is in this respect that infant baptism is valuable as a corrective to the danger inherent in the Baptist position (though not necessarily succumbed to) that too much stress will be placed on the human contribution: for in the baptism of an infant the grace of God for that person is manifestly and unmistakably prior to the individual's response of faith. There is, however, a risk in this that, because of the interval in time between the act of grace and the conscious profession of faith, both grace and faith will be conceived as impersonal quantities rather than as the divine and human sides of a personal encounter between God and man —and again the Baptists are right to warn against this. But there is no reason why infant baptism cannot be thought of as the beginning of an entirely personal relationship between God and the individual.

The loving Father is seeking out His child from his earliest days. That God plans to bring him to joyful acknowledgment of his heavenly Father is empirically clear from the fact that He has sent him in a Christian home.[32] The sacrament of baptism is a sign that God is graciously leading the child to faith and to a life that will exhibit both the fruits of repentance and the fruit of the Spirit in ethical conduct. Of course, infant baptism is not unfailing in its effect; but neither is it unknown for those baptized as adults to fall away—in the one case as in the other, man apparently continues to be free to reject the grace of God.

2. Every baptism is, in a measure, proleptic as well as actual in its effect. It is clear from St Paul that baptism marks the beginning of a new life of continuing obedience in the Spirit and constitutes a seal "unto a day of redemption". The practical implications of baptism must be unfolded all along the Christian life, and the full development will be reached only at the time of perfect salvation in the kingdom of the End. Viewed in this ethical and eschatological light, the question of the time of baptism, infant *versus* adult, recedes in importance. On the one hand, it may be argued that the sign of God's saving purpose for a man's life should be administered to him as soon as possible; on the other hand, the argument may be advanced that there is no true proleptic sign unless *both* the ultimately necessary partners, grace *and* faith, are brought into play. But in both cases baptism is regarded only as a beginning, and it is the end that counts.

3. We may question whether the baptism solely of professing believers does justice to the relation between the infant children of Christian parents and the people of the covenant. Under the Old Covenant, Jewish children were part of the people of God. It is not legitimate to draw an absolute distinction between an allegedly mere natural, national, or sociological initiation into the Jewish people and initiation into the supra-national and spiritual New Covenant which

can be entered only on the deliberate profession of faith. For Israel is part of the *Heilsgeschichte*, chosen by God for service in the salvation of mankind; and circumcision is a divinely given sign. The possibility must remain open that the children of Christian parents are *part of* the covenant people[33] and are not merely "specially related to the Body of Christ".[34]

Is it enough to say[35] that the children of Christian parents, as indeed all children, occupy an indisputable place in the love of Christ but are no more qualified for baptism thereby than are the other objects of Christ's affection, the sick, the helpless, the ignored, the despised? Is a service of blessing[36] based on Matt. 19: 13–15; Mark 10: 13–16; Luke 18: 15–17 sufficient embodiment of the place of children of Christian parents in the plan of God for His covenant people?[37] Or should not these infants receive baptism as the sign of initiation into the covenant people which acknowledges God's rule?[38]

4. The fourth argument starts empirically and ends theologically. In many Baptist churches in Britain it often happens that a person reared in a Baptist family comes to be admitted to Church membership upon profession of faith, without baptism being required at all. Is it for reasons of propriety that English adolescents and adults are reluctant to undergo baptism by total immersion? Neville Clark admits that "the Baptist communion bids fair to become the only major branch of the Christian church where baptism is not of universal observance—a somewhat curious basis from which to attempt to justify a separate denominational existence". The holy communion, the sacrament of the continuing life in the Church, is often given before, and even totally apart from, the sacrament of baptism which is the sign of initiation into the Church. This is almost bound to lead to an undervaluing of baptism: baptism can be postponed indefinitely or considered as an entirely optional extra. Is not infant baptism better than no baptism at all?

Some defences of infant baptism go so far in the direction of counter-attack as almost to suggest that paedobaptists oppose the baptism of professing believers *altogether* rather than the baptism *solely* of professing believers. Far from that, I would hold that baptism upon profession of faith gives the best possibility of embodying the full range of the gospel truths of salvation, but that infant baptism, though it has difficulties and dangers, is not without finding some justification in the biblical picture of salvation, that in certain historical circumstances it has played an appropriate role in Christian initiation, and that (finally) it may serve as a corrective to the dangers and difficulties that attend "believers' baptism". The Baptists have a strong case, but it is not so successful as to be exclusive:[39] there is a worthwhile case to be made for infant baptism also.

It may well turn out that both "believers' baptism" and also the varying patterns of initiation governed by infant baptism must all (each theologically justifiable, though in differing degrees) somehow be deliberately retained in any ecumenical pattern of initiation, with the circumstances of the Church in each particular place determining which is to preponderate, the baptism of the infants of Christian parents or the baptism of professing believers.

Rather than come to any would-be timeless theological conclusions on the matter, we should first see how Christian initiation takes its place in the present historical situation, in relation both to the movement towards churchly unity and also to the conditions in which the Church's mission has to be pursued; to these questions the next two chapters are devoted.

V

INITIATION AND UNITY

THE NEW TESTAMENT declares that "there is one baptism" (Eph. 4: 5)[1] and that "we are all baptized into one Body" (1 Cor. 12: 13). Baptism εἰς Χριστόν means that we "are all one man in Christ Jesus" (Gal. 3: 27–28). The entail of the oneness of Christ is the unity of baptism and the unity of the Church which is entered by baptism (cf. 1 Cor. 1: 10–13). It is not, then, surprising that the modern ecumenical movement should eventually, after at first simply accepting with gratitude the almost universal practice of baptism as at least one already given element of visible unity, decide on a more thorough theological investigation of the relation between baptism and the unity of the Church. If, some felt, the unity of baptism were shown to be intact, then the unity of the Church could not be far to seek. Recognition by the denominations of the oneness of baptism should lead to the sharing of the eucharist together,[2] and the visible unity of the Church, already thereby achieved in principle, would only need detailed elaboration.

The Commission of the World Council of Churches on Faith and Order devoted considerable attention in the 1950s to the theology of baptism itself; and it was gratifying to find Anglicans, Baptists, Congregationalists, Lutherans, Methodists, Orthodox, Presbyterians, and even a Quaker, subscribing in 1960 a report on *The Meaning of Baptism*[3] which saw baptism as rooted in the whole history of salvation and particularly in Jesus Christ, and which showed agreement on the benefits of salvation conferred in baptism. To the writers of the report it had, however, already become apparent that baptism offered no easy solution to the problem of Christian disunity. But even the diminished degree of optimism which their measure of agreement on the theology of baptism still allowed can, in fact, be maintained only at the cost of refusing to admit that the report failed to face squarely two major issues. The report tends to use "baptism" and "the Church" as though they were univocal terms,[4] but in fact these words pose two major questions with regard to Christian initiation in a divided Christianity:

1. *What "baptism" is it that conveys the benefits of salvation including membership of the Church?* There is "baptism" as administered to infants and considered theologically complete. There is "baptism" as given to infants and regarded as in some sense waiting for a personal confession of faith. There is "baptism" as administered to professing believers. Are these the one reality administered in three different forms, or are they three realities which simply have in common the water, the invocation of the Trinity and the appellation "baptism"? In other words, do water and the invocation of the Trinity suffice to make "baptism", to make the "one baptism", without regard to those other circumstances? To put it in directly ecclesiological terms: What is the composition of "the Church" into which baptism initiates a person? Does "the Church" include infants as full members, *or* does it allow progression to a new stage in membership when the person baptized as an infant comes to profess faith, *or* is "the Church" composed entirely of professed believers?

2. *How is a person's initiation related to the Church Universal, and how to a particular denomination?* This question needs to be put both in the case of baptism (however understood) and in the case of confirmation (however understood). And it is a question to which an answer must be given both by denominations which make an exclusive claim to be the "the Church" and also by denominations which believe that the Universal Church embraces others besides themselves.

The greater part of this present chapter will be devoted to examining the ways in which the various denominations answer these questions: it will reveal how the question of initiation is part and parcel of the whole problem of defining the Church when there is disunity among Christians. But before looking at the contemporary argument we glance at the problem of initiation in relation to Christian unity and disunity as it already confronted the ancient Church.

The scene of the major controversy shifted between North Africa and Rome. It arose in the third century when persons already baptized by the schismatic Novatianists sought admission to what won through as the continuing Catholic Church. Did their baptism by the Novatianists count as true baptism or should they now receive baptism at Catholic hands? Cyprian of Carthage, with epistolary support from Firmilian of Caesarea, held that Novatianist baptism was "no baptism", being administered outside the community of the Church in which alone the Holy Spirit dwelt.[5] But Stephen of Rome contended that the African Catholics should not *re*baptize, for "whoever is baptized in the name of Christ, no matter where, immediately obtains the grace of Christ".[6]

The Council of Arles (314) pronounced thus: "Concerning the Africans who use their own laws and rebaptize, the decision is that if anyone should come to the Church from heresy, they should ask him the creed and if they see that he was baptized in the Father and the Son and the Holy Spirit, let a hand only be imposed upon him so that he may receive the Holy Spirit. But if he should respond negatively to the question about the Trinity, let him be baptized."

Some have concluded that, while heretical or schismatic baptism into the Trinity was accepted by the Catholic Church, heretical "confirmation" (hand-laying for the gift of the Spirit) was not. Others believe, however, that the laying of hands on reconciled heretics or schismatics for the reception of the Spirit should be interpreted as the administration of penance, and not as a repetition of the post-baptismal hand-laying.[7]

It may be that there was a certain ambiguity about the hand-laying bestowed on reconciled heretics and schismatics in the West, since both penance and "confirmation" normally involved the imposition of hands and were said to give the Holy Spirit. To want to make a neat distinction between "confirmation" and "penance" in the case of converted heretics and schismatics may in fact be simply the result of looking at the matter from the viewpoint of the sacramental system in its later developments.

Augustine's solution to the problem of baptism administered by the Donatists amounted to saying that it was *valid* but *not efficacious* until the baptized person was reconciled to the Catholic Church.[8] Any distinction between validity and fruitfulness may raise its problems, but the extreme awkwardness involved in the plain *opposition* between the two in Augustine's would-be solution[9] is a clear indication that there is something radically amiss when Christian disunity renders it impossible for there to be a simple unclouded relation between the "one baptism" and the "one Church".[10]

Turning now to the present-day denominations, we look first at two which each make an exclusive claim to be the one true Church: the Roman Catholics, and the Orthodox. The Council of Trent in 1547 anathematized anyone who should deny that baptism given by heretics in the name of the Trinity and with the intention of doing what the Church does was true baptism (*verum baptismum*); and it appears to be the Roman position to acknowledge as valid *and efficacious* any baptism performed in water and with invocation of the Trinity[11] by any person having "the intention of doing what the Church does".[12] But it is precisely as *Catholic* (i.e. Roman Catholic) baptism that all such baptisms have been recognized: a person baptized in another denomination is treated as an individual "Catholic" who is refused "Catholic" communion only because he does not, through ignorance, acknowledge the universal jurisdiction of the Pope. It seems that a non-Roman Christian is an excommunicate member of "the Church", whose baptism may avail for salvation.

The difficulty with this view is that it gives a highly artificial account of any person who has never been in any practical sense a member of the Roman Catholic Church and, far from considering himself a lapsed and deprived Catholic, has found Christian fellowship in another body which *as a community* believes itself to be at least *part of* the Church Universal. There are, however, just the slightest of hints that Roman Catholics are beginning to undertake something of a reappraisal of their doctrine of the Church and its unity under the pressure of the modern ecumenical movement; and the question of baptism is bound to be involved in any shift in ecclesiology.

Since Leo XIII (1878–1903), Roman documents have referred with increasing affection to the Orthodox Churches as "the Eastern *Churches*", and some provisions of the decree *Orientalium Ecclesiarum* of the Second Vatican Council perhaps indicate that this appellation may now be regarded as granting them some measure of ecclesiological significance in their own right.[13] The decree *On Ecumenism* declares separated "Churches and churchly communities" (including communions stemming from the Reformation) to be *as communities* "not devoid of meaning and value in the mystery of salvation".

It looks as though Roman Catholic theologians must now ask themselves, not only about the relation of non-Roman baptism to the Roman Catholic Church, but also about the relation of non-Roman baptism certainly to the "Churches" or "communities" in which it is administered and even perhaps, if these "Churches" and "communities" are allowed any ecclesiological significance in their own right, to a Universal Church which is no longer identified exclusively with the *Roman* Catholic Church.

When welcoming these hints at a possible modification in the Roman Catholic doctrine of the Church, non-Romans should not forget that the decree of 1870 remains in force which makes the universal jurisdiction of the Pope *de fide*.

The Orthodox hold that baptisms performed outside the Orthodox fold are an anomaly, since the sacraments belong to the Church. Believing that they themselves have the authority of "the Church" to decide in the matter of the recognition of sacraments, the Orthodox invoke the double principle of "strictness" and "economy" and exercise discretion as to the best course to adopt in each case.[14] They exercise "economy" only when a convert comes to Orthodoxy, and the fact that a convert may not be required to receive baptism at Orthodox hands does not imply recognition of his baptism *before* he became Orthodox.[15]

There has been variety in the way in which the Orthodox have received converts from Western Churches. As a counter-blow to the proselytizing activity of the Latins, a Definition signed by the patriarchs of Constantinople, Alexandria and Jerusalem in 1755 decreed that converts to Orthodoxy should be *baptized* according to the Orthodox rite of triple immersion. This practice remained in force in the Greek Churches until the late nineteenth century and the early twentieth, when the Greeks returned to an earlier custom and contented themselves with a chrismation (apparently understood as exactly equivalent to that normally given directly after Orthodox baptism) of all Western converts (whether Catholic or Protestant). The eighteenth century saw the Russian Church, on the other hand, become more lenient in its practice. A Council at Moscow in 1620 had decreed that all converts must be baptized on embracing Orthodoxy, but the requirement was relaxed to chrismation for Roman Catholics in 1667 and for Protestants in 1718, and since 1757 the Russians have demanded only a profession of the Orthodox faith and penance before admitting a converted Roman Catholic. Though non-Orthodox Christians may be recognized as possessing varying measures of Orthodoxy, eucharistic communion is possible, from an Orthodox viewpoint, only when there is complete harmony in faith, life and episcopal ministry.

Possessing a radically different ecclesiology from the Roman or the Orthodox are those denominations which hold, with some differing emphases among themselves, that denominational disunity exists *within* the Church. Of these denominations we discuss first the ones which practise infant baptism: Anglicans, Congregationalists, Lutherans, Methodists and Reformed. How do they relate the baptism and "confirmation" (however understood) practised by the divided denominations to the unity of the Church? That they recognize all Christian baptism, by whomsoever administered and whether given to adults or to infants, as referring to the Church Universal appears certain; but there seems to be some difference as to whether, or how, a baptism is related *also* to the denomination in which it is performed.

For instance the 1963 Report on Conversations between the Church of England and the Methodist Church expects that "unconfirmed Anglicans" will not be admitted to communion in the Methodist Church when the two Churches are at the stage of intercommunion (p. 49), implying that Anglicans hold such a view of baptism's part in Church membership that the baptism of an infant stamps that person not only as a Christian but as an Anglican and subjects him to Anglican discipline. A similar view might be taken by most Lutherans and by many Presbyterians, in so far as they ascribe to baptism the decisive role in Church membership.

In Methodism and Congregationalism, however, it is a much more frequent view that baptism relates an infant to the Church Universal in some way, while a person's denominational allegiance begins more properly at "confirmation" when he is "made a member". The looseness of a person's attachment to a particular denomination between baptism and confirmation reflects the way in which the baptism of an infant is regarded as incomplete, in the process of making a Christian, until the person professes his own faith.

As an instance of this denominational voluntaryism, we point to the fact that the British Methodist service of infant baptism does not employ the term "Methodist" at all but speaks of "the Church" or of "the congregation of Christ's flock" or in other such universal phrases, whereas the service of confirmation refers to the Methodist Church and to the place it cherishes in "the Christian Church—one, holy, catholic and apostolic". The implication is that the person who was as an infant received in some sense into the Church Universal (it matters little in which denomination his baptism was given) is now choosing to exercise membership of the Church Universal within the Methodist Church.

Reference to the denomination at confirmation is by no means confined to Methodism, however. It is not unknown for Reformed and Lutheran Churches to expect a confession of denominational loyalty at that service; and they too would claim also that the person was being confirmed in the Church Universal.

Apart from the Anglicans, all the denominations we are now discussing would receive into their membership with little liturgical formality any person who had been baptized and confirmed in another denomination, though some would demand, in the case of converts from Roman Catholicism, an explicit renunciation of their former allegiance. Anglicans ask for such a renunciation on the part of Roman converts, but demand also of Protestants who have not been episcopally confirmed that they should receive confirmation from an Anglican bishop.

The major difficulty is that in one way or another all these denominations regard initiation as relating a person at one and the same time to the Church Universal and to a particular denomination, when in fact the very existence of *separated* denominations means that a person *cannot* at one and the same time belong to any particular denomination and be in fellowship with all parts of the Church Universal.

Their fundamental agreement on the ecclesiological principle that Christian disunity exists *within* the Church has made it possible, despite the differences in their understanding of the relation of baptism and confirmation to Church Universal and to denomination, for Anglicans, Methodists, Presbyterians and Congregationalists to unite in the Church of South India (1947). Does this Church offer a pattern for the understanding and practice of initiation which could unite the four denominations in other places?

Some Methodists and Congregationalists may feel that too much is ascribed to baptism in the case of infants in the service provided in the *Book of Common Worship* (1963). Over confirmation, Congregationalists, Methodists and Presbyterians may be satisfied, but "high" Anglicans must be disappointed. At union, all members in good standing of all the uniting Churches were recognized as members of the new Church, though only former Anglicans had received episcopal confirmation; nor does the new Church restrict confirming to the episcopate but allows confirmation to be administered by the presbyter in charge of the local congregation. The service of confirmation in the *Book of Common Worship* is, however, based on the twofold theme of Anglican confirmation: prayer for the Holy Spirit and imposition of hands, and subjective ratification of the baptismal covenant.

There are other Protestant denominations which, though holding that disunity exists *within* the Church, adopt a different position over the recognition of baptism in other denominations. I refer to the Churches of the believers' baptism movement, like Disciples, Brethren and Baptists. In the main, these allow that all *believers* are fellow-Christians with themselves and members of the Church Universal, even though they may have received only "infant sprinkling"; the baptism of believers is the sole true baptism.

The difficulty with this view is that it places, paradoxically enough for a *Baptist* movement, too little weight on baptism in the making of a Christian. It springs in part, no doubt, from the charitable desire not to unchurch the paedobaptists; but neither is it unconnected with the fact that many people reared in Baptist circles never seek baptism even when they come to believe, reckoning "faith" to be sufficient without the Dominical ordinance of baptism.

In very recent years, however, some scholars of the believers' baptism movement have made a constructive attempt to see the baptismal problem from the viewpoint of Church unity. Noteworthy studies include *The One Baptism* (St. Louis, 1960) by S. J. England, who is an American Disciple, and *Baptism Today and Tomorrow* (London, 1966) and *Baptism and Christian Unity* (London, 1966) by G. R. Beasley-Murray and A. Gilmore respectively, both English Baptists.

England claims to restate the traditional opinion of the Disciples: the basis for unity in baptismal practice is to be found in baptism by immersion upon profession of faith, since this alone (it is held) is *indisputably* present in the New Testament. All believers who have not been baptized in this way, though they are certainly Christians, should now submit to such baptism for the sake of churchly unity, just as in Acts, Cornelius and his friends, though already acceptable to God, were baptized in order that they might be brought into the unity of the institutional Church.

Less naïvely, Beasley-Murray[16] considers that any solution to the baptismal problem must take account of the existence (as he sees it) of *two* "baptisms" (infant and believer's) in current ecclesiastical practice. As present possibilities towards a solution, he calls on paedobaptists to reform their practice by tightening discipline against "indiscriminate baptism" and Baptists to reform theirs by demonstrating again in action the theological inseparability of baptism from conversion and Church membership.

Gilmore's conciliatory book makes the most of the common ground that can be shown to exist in the present generation between Baptist theologians and theologians of the paedobaptist (particularly Protestant) denominations. When, however, he characterizes infant baptism as "partial and defective, though nevertheless baptism" he concedes more than would most other equally ecumenically-minded Baptists.

Union schemes including denominations which baptize only professing believers are afoot in Ceylon, North India/Pakistan, New Zealand and Wales. Of these we select two, as examples: Wales and North India/Pakistan.

The Welsh scheme includes Presbyterians, Congregationalists, Methodists and Baptists. In its *Supplementary Report on Baptism* (1963), the committee of the four denominations proposed the following statement as a basis for agreement: "In view of the historical facts that the Congregationalists, the Presbyterians and the Methodists practise infant Baptism and believe that the practice should be continued, and that the Baptists practise Believers' Baptism and likewise believe that it should be continued, the United Church of Wales shall allow the practice of both forms of Baptism, and shall receive as members those who have been baptized and who have made a personal and public confession of faith in Christ. The United Church shall assure freedom of expression for the particular convictions of the different traditions."

It is easy to see why this coexistence of infant baptism and believers' baptism should not prove awkward for the Congregationalists, Methodists and Baptists: on the one hand, many Methodists and Congregationalists consider infant baptism as simply a declaration of the fact that Christ died for all and a rather undefined dedication of the child to God, and place far greater stress on the "Church membership" which is conferred upon profession of faith; while many Baptist churches, on the other hand, admit people to membership who have been baptized either as infants (in other denominations) or not at all. But one might have expected the Presbyterians, in so far as they stand in the Reformed tradition which elsewhere in the world expresses vehement opposition to anything that smacks to it of rebaptism, to have restricted the ready allowance of a person baptized in infancy to receive believers' baptism if he should later request it.[17]

In general, it may be said that these Welsh proposals depend far too much on the attitude, widely shared in the British Free Churches, that all "externals" are adiaphora and that what counts is "spiritual" unity, for them ever to be accepted as contributing much to the solution of the problem of "the one baptism" and "the one Church" on its worldwide scale.

In North India, for instance, the problem appears, by virtue both of the denominations concerned in the union negotiations and also of the position of the Church in Indian society, in a much more acute form. Anglicans are involved here, and there is a correspondingly greater awareness of the traditional view that baptism is unrepeatable, as well as of the part which baptism, even when administered to infants, plays in conferring the benefits of salvation, including membership of the Church. Again, Baptists, Disciples and Brethren in North India place believers' baptism and Church membership in a far closer relation than is often the case among Baptists in Britain. And finally, the Indian situation itself, in which Christians are clearly marked off from the rest of society means that baptism, whether of an infant or of an adult, occupies a much more important place in a person's life than it does in the lives of the British.

These factors, coupled with the recognition that Church union is a pressing need, have led to an excellent consideration, at once theologically serious and existentially committed, of the problem of "the one baptism" and "the one Church". No complete solution has yet been reached (indeed the Negotiating Committee in 1965 decided that the Plan of Union should be submitted to the denominations for decision in the recognition that what has proved the thorniest problem concerning initiation had not yet been given a satisfactory answer); but certain progress has been made.[18]

The proposed Plan of Union (now in its fourth edition, 1965) sets out two alternative patterns of complete initiation: the one being (*a*) infant baptism, (*b*) Christian nurture, (*c*) public confession of faith, (*d*) participation in communion; the other (*a*) infant dedication, (*b*) Christian nurture, (*c*) baptism upon profession of faith, (*d*) participation in communion. The form of "admission into communicant membership", whether of those baptized as infants or of those baptized as believers, is to include prayer for the gift of the Holy Spirit and the laying-on of hands by the bishop or presbyter. It is at this service also that one baptized in infancy makes his public profession of faith and "affirms his acceptance of the Baptism administered to him in infancy and recognizes in that Baptism the outward visible sign of the regenerating grace of God".

The thorniest problem concerns the procedure to be followed in the united Church when a person who has been baptized as an infant comes to be convinced that he must be baptized as a believer. In the eyes of paedobaptists, the granting of his request would strike at infant baptism in general and would contravene the traditional tenet that baptism is unrepeatable in the life of any one person.

The upholders of the baptism solely of professing believers, however, argue that the conscience of the person who requested "believer's baptism" in this way would have to be respected in the same way as they themselves would be respecting the conscience of paedobaptists by agreeing to a pattern of initiation dictated by infant baptism as one of the two alternative patterns in the united Church; nor would this be offending against the traditional view that baptism is unrepeatable, for infant baptism is not true baptism.

The third edition of the Plan of Union (1957) sought, in Appendix B, to give "guiding principles" for such a case in the united Church: but in the light of the continuing debate that Appendix has been omitted from the fourth edition, and the problem now belongs to those matters of difference about which the Lord would, it is confidently believed, reveal His will when those of diverse convictions met "in brotherly converse within one Church".

This practical question has already occasioned a significant theological examination of the traditional opinion that baptism is unrepeatable in the life of any one person. Anglicans and Baptists have both stuck to this opinion in the past. The difficulty, of course, is that they differ on whether this unrepeatable baptism can be given to infants.[19]

North India has asked: How, in the difficult case envisaged, can the deadlock be broken? One way is to challenge the unrepeatability of baptism. It is pointed out, first, that the chief scriptural text traditionally cited in its support, namely Eph. 4: 5, will not bear this meaning (see p. 98, note 1); and, secondly, that one of the decisive factors in the shaping of the traditional opinion was the ancient controversy over the recognition of heretical or schismatic baptism, whereas North India is faced with a different sort of issue, namely one consequent on the proposed existence of two different baptismal practices within the permitted limits of doctrine in the one Church.

There is considerable force in these points; but the weakness in making an absolute challenge to the unrepeatability of baptism lies in the way in which it opens up the possibility for a person to demand a baptism as often as he determines to "make a new start". This is a real danger in the case of the "perfectionist"; and it would be an affront to the almost universal Christian conviction, perhaps not quite exactly formulated in the traditional opinion that baptism is unrepeatable in any circumstances, that there is something of the once-for-all about baptism.

A better way therefore is to ask precisely what it is about baptism that is once-for-all: the unrepeatable thing may perhaps not be, in any simple sense, the water and the Threefold Name. This is the line of approach adopted, for instance, by the Methodist, J. C. Hindley.[20]

Hindley argues that "under our Plan we have accepted the place of personal conviction and profession of faith, in the fullness of initiation. Not only does a person receive the sacramental grace of God, but he may know that he has received it through conscious response."

The usual way for a believer to gain this assurance of his salvation is through his present experience of faith *plus* recollection of the fact that he has been baptized. But some people baptized as infants may come to the conviction that this assurance, which is what the Bible means by God's "seal" upon faith, is so closely linked with baptism in the New Testament that it can be conveyed only through a baptism administered to them after they have come to faith. This *need* not be regarded as casting doubt on any unrepeatable *objective effects* of a previous baptism in which the grace of God was bestowed even on an infant, but in the nature of things infant baptism cannot at the time when it is administered convey this assurance which is the due of every Christian *as part of his initiation.*[21] A "second baptism" might therefore be allowed in such difficult cases: the repetition of the act of baptism should be understood as *making known* to the person the saving activity which God had in fact already displayed towards him in the first act of baptism.

Objections to this suggestion can quickly be made: (1) Is it right to perform with purely *cognitive* intent an act which is normally credited with having *effective* value? And even if this question be answered in the affirmative, it is very difficult to see how repetition of the action of baptism, even though it were performed with only cognitive intent, could in practice avoid being looked on in a way derogatory to the objective effectiveness of the original baptism. (2) There seems to be something so fundamental about the traditional correlation (which is hard to define strictly) between a once-for-all-ness of baptism and the once-for-all-ness of the death and resurrection of Christ that to repeat the act by which a man is once made a sharer in Christ's death and resurrection has been understood by many (in a way which is perhaps more intuitive than logical) to strike at the sufficiency of the death once accomplished by Christ for his salvation or to be tantamount to crucifying Christ afresh.[22] (3) The Christian's continually repeated dying to self and rising to new life which is admittedly necessary *within* the baptismal life has, historically, found cultic expression in the sacrament of penance or in some non-sacramental type of confession,[23] but the Church has usually fought shy of any repeated ceremony with water that could appear to question the benefits of the original baptism;[24] moreover the eucharist, whose meal symbolism is well suited to repeatability, provides for the continually repeated appropriation of the benefits of Christ's death and resurrection.

Looked at closely, none of these objections carries absolute theological conviction, and therefore the way may be open for Hindley's proposal to be accepted. Yet the gravest hesitation must attend any flouting of the traditional opinion, which is firmly rooted in the historical practice and conscience of the universal Church even if it is not so logically watertight as to demand invariable adherence, that the unrepeatability of baptism is needed in order to match the unquestioned facts that God acted once-for-all in a decisive way in Christ, and that God acts once-for-all in a decisive way, no matter how much the person may backslide and need to repent, in the life of an individual. Hindley himself states that any "second baptism" must be regarded as *exceptional.*

Before leaving the question of initiation and Christian unity, we must at least glance at the problems presented by various groups which abandon all outward forms of initiation or substitute entirely new ceremonies for the traditional ones or introduce further requirements in the making of a Christian. Quakers and Salvationists have abandoned the traditional sacraments: Quakers have no rite of initiation, while Salvationists have a ceremony of enrolment under the Army flag. The World Conference on Faith and Order at Edinburgh in 1937 declared that "it is generally agreed that the united Church will observe the rule that all members of the visible Church are admitted by Baptism": what then would be the position of Quakers and Salvationists? Salvationists are not opposed to the traditional sacraments on principle, though they do not consider them necessary; some Salvationists might therefore submit to baptism. As to Quakers and unbaptized Salvationists, one suggestion is that they might be seen as constituting a continuing witness to the inward values of the faith which run the risk of being lost in outward forms.[25]

Pentecostalists, on the other hand, retain water-baptism and give it upon experience of "regeneration", whether or not a person has been baptized previously; they also believe that a separate "baptism with the Holy Spirit", preferably evidenced by glossolalia, is part of the normal pattern of a Christian's initiation.

Less of an institutional problem are those within the traditional Protestant Churches who minimize all outward forms (even though they observe them) and talk of the way in which they "became a Christian" at the moment when, possibly years after baptism and confirmation, they experienced one particular form of conversion in an entirely "spiritual" manner.

It has been made clear in this chapter that there has been no simple, unclouded relation between the "one baptism" and the "one Church" as long as there has been disunity among Christians and that none of the existing ecclesiologies can give a satisfactory account of the relation between the two in the present state of things.

Is there a way forward to the practical accomplishment of that perfect match between the one baptism and the one Church which theology demands? Certainly the diversity of understanding and practice just revealed forbids the taking of the simple fact that practically all denominations use water and the Threefold Name as a short cut to churchly unity. Yet some measure of optimism may still be in place if one looks to the origin and the goal of the sacrament of baptism. Baptism is a Dominical ordinance, and its ultimate aim is to incorporate men into the community of the final kingdom. May we not hope, now that divided Christians have come to show some measure of repentance for their separation, that the Lord will find some way of allowing His sacrament to work creatively for that healing of the divisions among Christians which will allow the Christian community to represent the first-fruits of the kingdom more perfectly and in a way which will win the world's conversion to His kingship?

In the next chapter we discuss the part which baptism is currently playing in the Church's mission of proclaiming the gospel of God's kingdom.

VI

INITIATION AND MISSION

BETWEEN THE times of God's inauguration of His kingdom in Jesus Christ and His ultimate fulfilment of that kingdom, the Church on earth shares in the mission of God to the world by proclaiming, through its words and deeds and very being, the good news of the kingdom. Sent to disciple all mankind to Christ, the Church baptizes in the name of the Trinity those who accept the gospel; and the baptized person himself becomes thereby a member of the baptizing community. Baptism both introduces one into the community which knows the benefits of salvation and also imposes on one the obligation of participating in the further prosecution of the saving mission. Proclamation leads to baptism: baptism leads to proclamation. In this chapter baptism is examined in the perspective of mission.[1]

Recent years have seen a rediscovery of the missionary obligation that baptism lays upon the Christian. Baptism is for the upbuilding of the Church which certainly has its own internal life and the joy of cultically sharing in the Son's worship of the Father in the Holy Spirit: but it belongs also to the Church on earth to share in God's mission to the world through the Son in the Holy Spirit; and baptism equally obliges the Christian to participate in that mission. The Orthodox have played an important part in the theological rediscovery of what one of them[2] calls "the cosmic significance" of baptism: the chrismation of the Orthodox baptismal complex is viewed as anointing all the faithful to the royal priesthood in Christ, which means that they act mediatorially between God and world by showing forth the excellencies of Him who called them out of darkness into His marvellous light (cf. 1 Pet. 2: 9).[3]

The Roman Catholic rediscovery of "the laity" as instruments of mission has found one of its theological bases in baptism as ordination to the royal priesthood, and the tag of Jerome is frequently noted: "Sacerdotium laici, id est baptisma";[4] while confirmation is seen by an increasing number of theologians as that part of the baptismal complex which confers the gift of the Holy Spirit for witness.

The study, *Ye are baptized* (Geneva, 1961), written by Dr L. Vischer for the Department on the Laity of the World Council of Churches, is an examination of the denominational liturgies of initiation in the light of this new awareness of baptism's "implications for the mission and service of church-members in the world".

One of the most recent writers on the subject is the Anglican, J. G. Davies, in his book, *Worship and Mission* (London, 1966). Baptism is there seen as grounded in the baptism of Jesus Christ (the inauguration of His mission) and in His death and resurrection (the culmination of His mission). Thus our baptism initiates us into the *missio Dei*, it is "a sacrament of identification, of suffering, of dying life poured out for others", it is a cultic act which is meant as the pattern of a whole life which reproduces the pattern of Christ's. The Spirit who anointed Christ for His mission (Luke 4: 18ff.) is given in baptism to Christians, in order that they may bear witness in the mission of God to the world (e.g. Acts 1: 8; 1 Pet. 1: 12).

It is all very well, and theologically proper to talk of the missionary obligation that baptism lays on a person, and one may even hope that this theological rediscovery will meet with an increasing practical response from "active Church members". But the empirical fact is that there are at the moment millions of baptized persons, baptized years ago in infancy, who have not the faintest existential notion of the worship, fellowship, service and mission involved in the Christian life; and the denominations of today add to their future number by continuing to baptize as infants people who stand perhaps even less chance of coming to personal commitment. When baptism is looked at in the perspective of mission, one of the most urgent issues is shown to be: *Whom* shall the Church baptize into the worshipping and missionary community which it represents?

Election lies ultimately in the mysterious will of God, and baptism and non-baptism are no final guarantee of salvation and damnation respectively: but it would be clean contrary to the New Testament to pretend that there was meant to be anything but a very close correspondence, if not identity, between the baptized and the truly Christian. If the Church is to be a faithful steward of the divine sacraments, then it must consider carefully the question of who shall be given baptism.

A glance at history reveals that there are two classical types of situation with regard to baptism and mission. The one is that in which the gospel is proclaimed for the first time in new territory; there the *norm* is the baptism of the adult believer who has accepted the gospel he hears, though from very early times, if not from the apostolic age itself, his children are often baptized *also*, in order that they may enjoy the benefits of salvation with their parents. The other situation is that of the "Christian society" in which generation after generation grows up in the faith proclaimed over them from birth and it is almost unthinkable that any person should be a deliberate unbeliever; there the norm, historically and in many cases theologically, has been the baptism of infants.

The Western Church is confronted with an increasing number of people who, usually still baptized in infancy, either have never accepted the gospel in later years or, having gone so far as to be confirmed in adolescence, have now lapsed from the eucharistic community.[5] Faced with proclaiming the gospel in a rapidly melting Christendom, is it perhaps to the field of what the Germans call "heathen-mission" that the Western Church must look for guidance in its baptismal practice at home?

When the Church's mission is being pursued in some Asian or African society which has never before heard the gospel, then baptismal practice follows the pattern of "first generation" practice in the New Testament and all the features of the New Testament theology of baptism mentioned in chapter I are dramatically realized:

1. *Christological reference.* It is baptism which stamps a person as Christ's man. W. Freytag[6] cites vernacular baptismal names such as "He has accepted me" from East Africa, "A new man" from Papua, "One has died for me" and "I have been rescued".

2. *Ecclesiological reference.* Baptism makes a person a member of a community whose distinctness is often shown by the enmity displayed towards it by the surrounding society. A baptized person is frequently ostracized by his natural family even though they may have tolerated him while he was a simple hearer of the gospel or reader of the Bible; an Indian baptismal ceremony may be watched by hissing villagers. The baptized becomes a member of a community in which divisions of caste or tribe count for nothing as all eat at the same Lord's Table.

3. *Eschatological reference.* Again this may be illustrated by baptismal names. H. W. Gensichen[7] quotes the following from the Chagga Christians of East Africa: "Wait for the life", "Wait for the joy", "I will not die". When Gensichen reports that an East African woman died with the words, "I now go to Him whom I saw in baptism", one is reminded of Thecla's words of old as she threw herself into the water when facing martyrdom in the arena, "In the name of Jesus Christ I baptize myself for the last day."[8] The frequent desire of converted

parents that their children should receive baptism with themselves is to be understood as due in part to the eschatological import of baptism: baptism has to do with ultimate salvation.

4. *Ethical reference.* That baptism is known to impose obligations of communal and personal behaviour which may mark a person off from his non-Christian neighbours is shown by the requests made to missionaries for "de-baptism" before undertaking an action contrary to Christian discipline. The ethical reference is illustrated also in the way in which a barren woman, often despised in pagan societies, is treated as an equal member of the baptized community.

5. *The priority of grace and the need for faith.* Where baptism cuts a person off from his previous social environment it is not an act lightly undertaken. A firm human decision is demanded for what the New Testament pictures as a change of lordship: the *apotaxis* of the ancient baptismal liturgies has its counterpart in the baptismal name from Papua, "I have thrown away", and the old *syntaxis* in vernacular names like "Stay by God" and "I hold fast to Him". In heathen-missions the fundamental practice is the baptism of adults in which this decision is demanded, but the convert has no doubt as to the priority of grace in the proclamation of the gospel, in the stirring of his faith, in his baptismal catechesis and in baptism itself. Baptism is God's act, a "visible word" of His that even the simple can understand.

If these New Testament baptismal truths are so well embodied[9] in the missionary practice of the Church in pagan societies, then we may well find help in Asia and Africa for the problem of who shall be baptized in our Western situation of a disappearing Christendom. The Church of South India, for instance, is quite firm on this point: "Candidates able to answer for themselves must be well instructed in the Christian faith and way of life and approved by the minister and the representatives of the congregation before they are brought to baptism. . . . Only those who are baptized and in good standing may bring their children for baptism."

Before turning to the situation of the Church in the West, however, let us look at a land which, once part of Christendom, has moved much further towards presenting a heathen-missionary environment for the Church than is yet the case in the Western world: I mean East Germany.

In East Germany[10] the pressure of conformism which kept the overwhelming majority of the population, largely estranged from the living faith, in a formal membership of the institutional Church exercised only through the ceremonial of baptisms, confirmations, weddings and funerals has under communist rule been replaced by the pressure of a new State-engendered conformism which drives the citizen to seek security through participation in a political cult of socialist "name-giving ceremonies", socialist "youth dedication", socialist marriages and socialist funerals. The worker, who in any case used to find baptism practically incomprehensible, now finds his need for a ceremony at the birth of his child met by the Party: and it needs a committed and courageous Christian father to bring his infant to the Church for baptism when he knows that he will thereby render himself politically suspect and jeopardize his prospects of promotion at work. Consequently the problems posed by the vast numbers of purely nominal Christians who still demand baptism for their children in the melting Christendom of the West are in East Germany well on the way to disappearing.

That the process is not taking place faster is due to the fact that after several years of debate the Church has now decided that an infant may be both "named" at a communist ceremony and baptized in the congregation and that it will confirm adolescents who have attended the communist *Jugendweihe*.[11] Even so the trend is irreversibly set towards the baptism of the infants of genuinely Christian parents only, and there is even pressure from some theologians in favour of pointing out to genuinely Christian families that baptism may be postponed until an adult age, the children being meanwhile commended to the congregation for prayer and Christian nurture.

What then about the Church in Western Europe, and what about Britain in particular?[12] There is an undeniable fall in the number of infants being baptized. To take the Church of England as an example: from the 1956 figure of 602 infant baptisms per 1,000 live births in the total population there was a sharp and consistent decline to 531 in 1962. Yet the great majority of parents still seek baptism for their infants in one denomination or another. Ministering on a Liverpool city housing estate taught me that the attitude of mothers who demand baptism for their children may range from the hesitantly magical, "It might bring him a bit of luck", to the firmly sacramental, "They come on better after they've been done". Baptism is accompanied by old wives' tales about what it is not proper for mother and child to do until they have been, respectively, churched and christened.

In the face of an almost complete lack of understanding of the Christian life on the part of most parents, few ministers are yet prepared to withhold baptism from the children. Some ministers would justify their readiness to baptize all and sundry on the ground that "all children have a right to baptism" or, more sophisticatedly, on the ground of the "objective redemption" accomplished by Christ's death for all men; but it was seen above (p. 53) that this depends on a defective view of baptism. Other ministers, while reluctant to refuse baptism, are nevertheless extremely exercised in their consciences by the state of "baptismal disgrace" as A. R. Vidler[13] called it in a pungent phrase as long ago as 1940.

If fewer and fewer people in Britain know the fundamentals of the Christian faith, can it be that the Church in Britain is being called to formulate and practise a baptismal discipline after the stamp of that observed in "overseas missions"? The evidence seems to be pointing in that direction, but before leaping to that conclusion it is necessary to pay heed to a caveat.

H. J. Margull[14] has pointed out that when the leaders of the World Council of Churches at the Amsterdam Assembly in 1948 and afterwards drew a simple parallel between "the missionary situation in Western Europe" and "the missionary situation in Asia or Africa" they were making things too easy for themselves theologically. A society in which the gospel has once been preached is not, even though the majority of the people then fall away from personal faith, the same as a society in which the gospel has never been preached at all. Amid all the general dechristianization of Western Europe, certain Christian values persist in society, and there are millions of people who, though they do not profess the fundamental Christian faith, nevertheless *have been baptized*. Missionary and baptismal practice must, for the moment, take into account the fact that the "Christian society" has still not entirely disappeared in the West. Margull's point is important; and in this time of *crisis for baptism*[15] the varying suggestions proposed, and experiments tried in baptismal practice, do in fact reflect the degree to which their authors consider Britain to have gone in the process of dechristianization.

The majority of practical experiments imply that their authors believe Britain to be still enough of a Christian country for the baptismal problem to be treated as *pastoral* rather than as *strictly missionary*. By this I mean that their approach is designed to *recall* to lapsed parents *the faith which they are already supposed to know*. The baptism of an infant is made the opportunity for teaching the parents more about the meaning of their own baptism, in the hope that they may be recalled to a living faith and bring up their children in the Christian way. Parents are visited in their homes, classes are held for instruction, and a rehearsal of the ceremony may take place on the preceding Sunday. An outstanding Anglican pastor, E. W. Southcott, while he was vicar of Halton, Leeds, used to keep four great occasions each year as the times of administering baptism to large numbers of children.[16] The Methodist Church in Notting Hill puts baptism at the centre of the 11 o'clock Sunday morning service once a month.[17] Mgr. J. Buckley[18] pleads for a restoration of the font's dignity in the parish church and for a real "celebration" of baptism to replace the hole-and-corner method of administration.

Though it may produce good results in the lives of some parents, this pastoral approach carries two dangers with it: it seems to underestimate the amount of instruction needed before many parents have even an inkling of the meaning of baptism, whether their own or the baptism they want for their children; it may also have a flavour of "using" both baptism and infant for the putative benefit of the parents when there is still really very little chance that the child will grow to a personal faith. It seems to me that a more rigorous approach is needed to match the degree of dechristianization already in evidence.

If the baptism of infants is ever right (and we have argued in chapter IV that it may be so), then it is surely right in the case of the children of parents who are in the eucharistic life of the Church. Many Anglican priests are at least moving towards the restriction of infant baptism to such cases when they enforce the canonical requirement of 1604 that the infant must have *godparents* who themselves have been admitted to the communion of the Church; but this restriction loses its effectiveness on account of the large number of confirmed Anglicans who, though having now lapsed from communion, are nevertheless willing to act as godparents for children of equally non-communicant, often unconfirmed, though usually baptized friends.

A discipline which restricted infant baptism to the children of communicant parents would do much to remove the scandal of the disparity between the great number of baptisms administered and the small number of eucharistic Christians. There is, I suppose, some slight danger that such a discipline might blackmail the ineradicably superstitious into temporary communion. A more serious difficulty is that even birth to genuinely Christian parents may perhaps no longer be looked on as sufficient indication that a person is likely to come to the faith demanded by his baptism: the general loosening of the pattern of family life in our society, and the comparative failure of the Church in the Christian education of the young, make it questionable whether generation will succeed generation in the faith. It may be preferable to postpone baptism even in the case of infants born to communicant parents.

It is important to note that advocacy of the postponement of baptism has not been confined to crypto-Baptists on the left wing of paedo-baptist denominations. It was, for instance, three "high churchmen" who signed the minority schedule published in *Baptism and Confirmation Today* (London, 1955), the final document produced by the Joint Committees of the Anglican Convocations of Canterbury and York. They propose an order for the making of a catechumen which "may be used, as well for an infant as for one who is able to answer for himself, and in particular, if the parents so desire, for one in whose case baptism has been deferred"; postponement of baptism would have the advantage of allowing baptism, confirmation and first communion to be administered as a united complex in later years. Again, J-J. von Allmen of Neuchâtel holds the view that the *best* solution to the baptismal problem would be an "admission to the catechumenate" in infancy and a full baptismal service at a later date with confession of faith, water baptism and hand-laying followed by communion.

There would indeed be three major gains in such a pattern:

1. Confession of personal faith would be clearly seen to belong with baptism since the two would come at the same point in the initiation complex.

2. First communion would take its proper place directly after baptism as the first enjoyment of that regularly renewed eucharistic participation in Christ which must follow on the once-for-all incorporation into Him at baptism.

3. Admission to the catechumenate would provide something of an answer to the problem of the relation of the children of Christian parents to the Church. To be a catechumen is to be pledged for baptism: one is proleptically a member of the Church. This idea seems to outcrop at various points in ancient sources: in the *Missale Gothicum* and the *Missale Bobbiense*, for instance, the service generally entitled "For the Making of a Catechumen" is called "For the Making of a Christian", and in the *Bobbiense* a threefold insufflation is given *to the catechumen* with the words, "Receive the Holy Spirit; mayest thou guard him in thy heart"; James of Edessa (+708) reveals that when, in an earlier day than his own, the catechumenate stretched over a long period, the catechumens were already called Christians;[19] the fifth-century Afri-

can bishop Quodvultdeus used the following image to catechumens: "You are not yet born anew in baptism, but you have been conceived in the Church's womb by the sign of the cross."[20] Moreover the giving of a name, or at least its registration, belongs in tradition more properly with the catechumenate than with baptism itself: and the naming of a child at his admission to the catechumenate would satisfy the parental sense that a child's name is an important part of his personality[21] and indicate that he is an individual who receives the loving address of God and of the Church.[22]

It would be important that admission to the catechumenate should not be used as a second-class ceremony to fob off those parents whom the minister judged unsuitable to have their infants baptized.[23] A more positive value should be attached to it, and in this way: in view of the indeterminate nature of the New Testament position, both historically and theologically, on the baptism of infants, and of the overwhelming ecclesiastical tradition in favour of infant baptism, it would be wrong (it seems to me) for the Church to refuse to baptize the infants of eucharistic parents even for the sake of the more effective prosecution of the Church's mission in particular historical cirumstances; but if a significant number of *such* parents could be encouraged to have their infants admitted to the catechumenate with a view to their *later* baptism, they would be making an extremely valuable witness in the situation of a melting Christendom to the fact that the full Christian life demands a firm decision of personal faith.[24] The greatly increased number of baptisms upon profession of faith which would (it is hoped) result from this practice in some years' time would be a powerful factor in the recovery by Western Christians of the biblical truth that the Church is a *distinct society*, called out of the world for God and sent by God into the world to proclaim His Kingdom for the world's salvation.

CONCLUSION

DOES THE foregoing survey allow us to see how an ecumenical pattern of initiation might take shape? I mean a pattern which, because it is faithful to the gospel "according to the Scriptures" and learns from the varied experience of the whole Christian people down the centuries, will first make for and then express the visible unity of the Church, and will at both stages aptly serve the Church's participation in the mission of God for the world's salvation.

The New Testament witness sets out the theological principles which must govern such a pattern. Liturgical initiation should bring out the primary work of Father, Son and Holy Spirit in the salvation which it sacramentally mediates; it should give a proper place to the human response for which God calls from those with whom He deals graciously; it should express the way in which the Christian life already represents in the midst of the world the first-fruits of the final kingdom in that it is a life of righteousness in the unity of the Body which tastes by anticipation the joy of the age to come.

Let us see how the three main patterns of initiation which history has bequeathed to the present stand up to judgment by this canon. (Forsaking descriptive accuracy for the sake of verbal economy I now call them the Eastern, the Western and the Baptist patterns.)

In administering the whole rite of initiation to infants, the Eastern practice shows most clearly the priority of God's action in the salvation of each individual, the divine primacy which the Eastern Fathers see exemplified in the passive formula "Baptizatur . . .". Moreover, the giving of first communion in immediate succession to baptism-chrismation demonstrates that the gifts and obligations of salvation conferred through baptism are to be renewed all along the Christian life through the sacrament of the eucharist. But this Eastern pattern suffers perennially from the defect of excluding any *real* profession of personal faith at the time of initiation. And in our time in particular it cannot count on either of the sets of socio-ecclesiological presuppositions which may justify this anticipation of the child's future response—those of a total

"Christian society" or those of a compact Christian community distinct from its non-Christian environment.

The Western pattern shares, through infant baptism, the Eastern emphasis on the priority of God's work in the salvation of each individual. On the other hand, no matter how much certain Roman, Lutheran, Anglican or Reformed theologians may insist on the sufficiency of infant baptism for Church membership, the continuing theological attempts to justify—after its more or less accidental beginning in the Middle Ages—the withholding of communion until later years, betray an underlying sense that initiation is not really complete until the individual is able to make a personal response of faith to God's saving approach. In the Protestant stream, this first real profession of personal faith finds liturgical expression in the delayed "confirmation" inherited from the Middle Ages and given this new content as its main theme. In the Catholic stream, the interpretation of this delayed "confirmation" chiefly as conferring a gift of the Holy Spirit distinct from the baptismal gift is perhaps rooted in a sense that at least the existential awareness of the Spirit's presence waits for the age of reason.

Taken as a whole, and optimistically, the Western tradition might seem to be a good embodiment of the truths both of God's priority in the work of individual salvation and also of the need for human response before initiation is complete. But this is achieved only at the cost of that splitting of the initiation complex which, as we saw in the third chapter, causes so many theological difficulties in the interpretation of the relations among the various parts. These difficulties are heightened at a time when the sociological phenomenon of a disappearing Christendom means that many are given baptism as infants who never come to profession of faith and the communicant life.

In the form in which it has been practised by Baptists, the Baptist pattern presents considerable drawbacks: first, the God-to-man movement in baptism has been neglected in favour of emphasis on the human confession of faith; secondly, the *exclusive* insistence on believers' baptism has not done justice, either to the distinct possibility (this is how I would rate the historical evidence) that infant baptism was practised in the apostolic age, or to the theological values which the Eastern and Western traditions have found in infant baptism; thirdly, Baptists have been embarrassed to find liturgical expression for the place occupied by children in the covenant people; lastly, baptism has not infrequently been omitted altogether from the process of becoming a member of the Church and has on these occasions disappeared as the normal sacramental foundation of the continuing communicant life.

Yet at bottom the Baptist pattern offers the best possibility of a unified initiation complex in which the divine and the human roles in the work of salvation are suitably expressed. Both because of the theological malaise which it finds in correlating the various elements of its own split pattern of initiation, and also because of the pastoral and missionary problems which that pattern causes in a melting Christendom, the West is open for the spread of the Baptist pattern; and this is to be welcomed, provided that in entering into the Baptist heritage the Western denominations may also bring the positive contributions which their own experience has taught them and which may remedy the weaknesses which the Baptist denominations have exhibited.

The following modifications might then be made in the Baptist pattern compared with the way in which Baptists have actually practised it: first, the God-to-man movement in the sacrament might be re-emphasized so that in the work of salvation the "by grace" of Eph. 2: 8 might be expressed as well as the "through faith"; secondly, if paedobaptists did not make an absolute theological renunciation of their past tradition but only recognized that they now found believers' baptism a better pattern (at least in the present circumstances), then the Baptist pattern would lose that *exclusive* character which implies, in a consistent sacramental theology, that those baptized as infants have no place in the visible Church; thirdly, the children of communicant parents might be liturgically admitted to the catechumenate in their infancy, for such a rite would show that they had at least a provisional place in the covenant people and thereby express a truth for which infant *baptism* is perhaps too strong an expression; fourthly, the use of hand-laying or unction *immediately* after the water would satisfy those who see New Testament evidence for two distinct "moments" in the normal baptismal event and could in any case act as a liturgical focus for the Pneumatological reference that, theologically, inescapably accompanies the Christological reference of baptism; finally, first communion might be restored to its place as the bridge between baptism and continuing participation in the eucharistic life of the Church.

Am I then advocating the adoption of a fundamentally Baptist pattern as *the* ecumenical pattern of initiation? No. Rather I confine myself to advocating the progress of a movement (whose first signs are just appearing) that will bring a modified Baptist pattern into greater and greater prominence. Though holding that a Baptist pattern with the modifications outlined in the previous paragraph would be the *best* pattern of initiation and should rightly dominate the overall picture, my hope, and certainly my expectation, is that such a pattern would not oust the Eastern and the Western altogether. My expectation is governed by a sober assessment of what is really likely: for of course one cannot imagine either the Eastern or the Western traditions being ready to give up at once or entirely their long customary practices in favour of a Baptist pattern. My hope is determined by an *inclusive* view of Christian unity, according to which the variety of practice that has been apparent through most of history and dates perhaps from the New Testament age itself allows for the counterbalancing, within a single whole, of one side of the often paradoxical truths of salvation by the other—so that, for instance, the continuing baptism of infants, which will surely take place in certain circumstances and which no Baptist argument has yet shown to be finally indefensible, will serve to offset the special danger to which a Baptist pattern seems always exposed by pointing to not just the necessity but the *priority* of God's work in the case of every individual salvation.

The changing pattern which I see already beginning, and whose promotion I would encourage, is ecumenical at least in so far as, seeking to adhere to Scripture and to the best of Christian Tradition (judged by the gospel to which the apostolic writings bear normative witness), it is *moving towards* a pattern acceptable to all the presently divided denominations, and suited to the Church's better participation in God's mission for the establishment of his kingdom in the world as it is now developing.

It would be foolish to think that the movement envisaged would be other than difficult in the extreme, and that for several reasons. First, the tremendous pressure of past custom will make change painful in all the denominations. Secondly, to ask Baptists to accept positively the continued existence of infant baptism is to demand, if not a surrender, then at least a radical re-interpretation of a *theological* principle hitherto held under the form of an exclusive insistence on believers' baptism—whereas paedobaptists, no matter how great would be the upheaval in their midst, would in the last resort be making only *practical* alterations; but Baptists might perhaps be prepared to pay this price for the spread of believers' baptism in ecclesiastical areas where infant baptism has long held sway. Thirdly, work still needs to be done on the difficult problem of possible "second baptisms" in a mixed practice in which infant baptism and believers' baptism are real alternatives. Finally, as long as we are only in the transitional stage of moving towards Church unity the problem remains, as we saw in the fifth chapter, of the dual relation of any pattern of initiation to "the Church" and to the still separated denominations. Nevertheless we are bold enough to hope that God's help will not fail as the Church strives earnestly to allow the divinely appointed means of salvation to play their proper role in the establishment of the kingdom.

NOTES

INTRODUCTION

1. For the Church of England, see the reports of the Joint Committees of Convocations, *Confirmation Today* (1944), *Baptism Today* (1949), *Baptism and Confirmation Today* (1955); the report of the Archbishops' Theological Commission, *The Theology of Christian Initiation* (1948); and the rites unsuccessfully proposed by the Liturgical Commission in 1958. The Church of Scotland's Special Commission on Baptism produced reports annually between 1955 and 1962 and a new order of infant baptism was first issued for experimental use in 1963.

I

THE NEW TESTAMENT THEOLOGY OF INITIATION

1. *Die kirchliche Lehre von der Taufe*, Zollikon-Zürich, 1943; E.T., *The Teaching of the Church regarding Baptism*, London, 1948.
2. E.T., *Baptism in the New Testament*, London, 1950.
3. *Baptism in the Thought of St Paul*, Oxford, 1964.
4. See the illustrations in the article, "Baptême de Jésus", in *Dictionnaire d'archéologie chrétienne et de liturgie*, vol. II, col. 346–380.
5. E.g. Flemington, pp. 105–109. Among earlier writers who regard Christ's Baptism as instituting Christian baptism are Chrysostom (*In Matth. Hom.* XII, 3; PG 57, 206), Ambrose (*In Luc.* II, 83; PL 15, 1583) and Thomas Aquinas (S.T. III, 66, 2).
6. "Thou art (this is) my beloved Son; with thee (in whom) I am well pleased": the great majority of commentators take the words of the voice from heaven at Mark 1: 11; Luke 3: 22; (Matt. 3: 17) as echoing both the messianic Psalm 2: 7 and the Servant song Isa. 42: 1. Cullmann (E.T. pp. 16–18) believes the original reference is solely to Isa. 42: 1, υἱός having crept into the Greek version because of its affinity with παῖς, the correct rendering of *abdi* (my servant); against this, however, must be set the Western text at Luke 3: 22 and the further uses of Ps. 2: 7 as a proof-text for Christ's royal Sonship at Acts 13: 33; Heb. 1: 5; 5: 5.
7. See, e.g., Cullmann, p. 19, and Flemington, pp. 31f., 123.

8. Cullmann (pp. 18f.) finds in this thought the clue to the puzzling phrase "to fulfil all righteousness" in Matt. 3: 15.

9. The verb used at Mark 1: 10; Matt. 3: 16, ἀναβαίνω, is frequently applied to the Ascension in the New Testament.

10. E.g. Cullmann, pp. 19–22; J. A. T. Robinson, "The One Baptism as a Category of New Testament Soteriology", *Scottish Journal of Theology* 6 (1953), pp. 257–74.

11. So, on Eph. 5: 25–27, T. Preiss, "Le Baptême des enfants et le Nouveau Testament", in *Verbum Caro* 1 (1947), pp. 113–22. According to the Church of Scotland study document *The Biblical Doctrine of Baptism* (1958), the "once-for-all baptism of the Church in Spirit at Pentecost" gave the Church a share in the "once-for-all baptism of Christ in blood on the Cross" and led at once to that preaching of the gospel to all creatures which "in turn leads to the baptism of individuals".

12. E.g. R. E. O. White (pp. 371–73); G. R. Beasley-Murray (pp. 45–67; 201–3).

13. *Infant Baptism in the First Four Centuries*, London, 1960, p. 23.

14. *Worship in the New Testament*, 1961, p. 50.

15. For Wesley's views see J. R. Parris, *John Wesley's Doctrine of the Sacraments*, London, 1963, pp. 35–61.

16. In *Baptism in the New Testament* (A. George *et al.*), pp. 115–58.

17. See Hippolytus, *Apostolic Tradition*, 21; Cyril, *Myst. Cat.*, II, 4; Ambrose, *De sacramentis*, II, 7, 20; *De mysteriis*, 4, 21; 5, 28.

18. Most of the Oriental Churches use the passive formula, though the Coptic and Ethiopic, like the Western rites, use the active. Too great an argument should not be based on the silence, but the earliest certain witnesses to an indicative formula are John Chrysostom (*Huit Catéchèses baptismales*, ed. A. Wenger, in *Sources chrétiennes*, 50, Paris, 1957, p. 147) and Theodore of Mopsuestia (*Les homélies catéchétiques de Théodore de Mopsueste*, edd. R. Tonneau and R. Devreesse, Città del Vaticano, 1949, pp. 403, 431–33); in the West certain evidence dates only from the seventh or eighth centuries. (But see E. C. Whitaker, "The History of the Baptismal Formula", in *Journal of Eccl. History* 16 (1965), pp. 1–12.)

19. Many ancient fonts have hexagonal and octagonal shapes in their design, in token of Christ's death on the sixth day of the week and his resurrection on the eighth, the first of a new week. On this and other symbolism in fonts and baptisteries, see J. G. Davies, *The Architectural Setting of Baptism*, London, 1962.

20. *Die Taufe: eine genetische Erklärung der Taufliturgie*, Innsbruck, 1958.

21. Edd. Tonneau and Devreesse, pp. 403, 441–43.

22. See H. Kirsten, *Die Taufabsage: eine Untersuchung zu Gestalt und Geschichte der Taufe nach den altkirchlichen Taufliturgien*, Berlin, 1960.

23. Cyril, *Myst. Cat.*, IV, 8; Ambrose, *De mysteriis*, 7, 34.

24. Introduced in 1951.

25. See, e.g., Cyril, *Myst. Cat.*, III: Christians are properly called χριστοί, because they have been anointed, through the symbol of the holy ointment, with the Holy Spirit wherewith Christ was anointed at His Baptism.

26. On the crown as an eschatological symbol see J. Daniélou, *Primitive Christian Symbols*, London, 1964, pp. 14–24.

27. Published London, 1946. Dix had already expressed similar views in his pamphlet, *Confirmation, or the Laying on of Hands?*, London, 1936; and K. E. Kirk had taken a similar line in criticizing the first interim report of the Joint Committees of Canterbury and York on the Administration of Baptism and Confirmation.

28. Faith and Order Commission Paper No. 29, printed in *One Lord, One Baptism*, S.C.M. Studies in Ministry and Worship, London, 1960.

29. Of the other texts, John 3 : 5 is severely mauled by many hands for differing purposes; on 1 Cor. 6: 11 M. Thurian (*La Confirmation*, p. 21) makes the gratuitous suggestion that the "washing" took place in the water baptism "in the name of the Lord Jesus Christ", whereas the "sanctification" took place in a distinct Spirit baptism ("in the Spirit of our God"), while "justification" sums up the full salvation accomplished in the two baptisms; in Gal. 4: 6, Thornton (pp. 11–13) saw our adoption as sons and God's sending forth of the Spirit into our hearts as two distinct stages in our initiation.

30. Leenhardt (p. 37f.) and M. Barth (pp. 141–45) also see a separation between baptism and the giving of the Spirit in this verse; but they interpret it, not as an argument in favour of "confirmation", but as an indication that God is not constrained by the baptismal rite to give the Spirit *hic et nunc*.

31. To this day the formula at chrismation in the Byzantine rite is "The seal of the gift of the Holy Spirit".

32. E.g. the Catholics, B. Neunheuser (*Taufe und Firming*, p. 23) and T. Marsh (in "The History and Significance of the Post-Baptismal Rites" in the *Irish Theological Quarterly* 29 (1962), pp. 175–206). Basil the Great expressly denies that the rite of chrismation rests directly upon the warrant of Scripture (*Spir.* 27, 66; PG 32, 188).

33 "Entry into Membership of the Early Church" in *Journal of Theological Studies* 48 (1947), pp. 25–33.

34. Dix alleges that the rite is reflected in 1 Cor. 10: 1ff. also, where the cloud (=*shekinah*), the sea and the manna and the water from the rock prefigure the gift of the Spirit, water baptism and the eucharist.

35. The evidence is to be found in R. H. Connolly, *The Liturgical Homilies of Narsai*, Cambridge, 1909, pp. xlii–xlix; cf. the discussions in B. Botte, "Le baptême dans l'Eglise syrienne" and A. Raes, "Où se trouve la confirmation dans le rite syro-oriental?" in *L'Orient syrien* 1 (1956), pp. 137–55, 239–54. That the prebaptismal anointing was believed to convey the Spirit is clear from *Apostolic Constitutions*, III, 16, 4 and VII, 22, 2 (ed. F. X. Funk, I, pp. 211, 406).

36. Scholars are wary of putting too much weight on the imposition of

hands in Acts 9: 10–19, since there is the complicating factor of the restoration of Paul's sight. The case of Cornelius (Acts 10f.) is to be seen as an instance of the Spirit's freedom to descend before the administration of any rite at all, and it is only by devious argumentation that this story of the first Gentile convert can be made to support the theory of two distinct moments in the normal initiation rite.

37. Pp. 104–25.

38. *Taufe und Firmung*, Freiburg i. B., 1956, pp. 1–23.

39. E.g. Cyril of Jerusalem, *Myst. Cat.*, III, 1; Theodore of Mopsuestia (ed. Tonneau and Devreesse, p. 457); Hilary of Poitiers, *Comm. in Matth.*, 2, 6 (PL 9, 927); Rabanus Maurus, *De cler. inst.* I, 28 (PL 107, 312–13). Among the moderns: Dix, *The Theology of Confirmation . . .*, p. 30; Thornton, pp. 101, 139f.; Thurian, *La Confirmation*, pp. 33f.

40. The distinction is clear in Luke; but with Mark much hinges on the force of *καὶ εὐθύς* in 1: 10.

41. Dix, p. 30; Thornton, p. 179; Thurian, pp. 23, 32; P. Evdokimov, *L'Orthodoxie*, Neuchâtel/Paris, 1959, p. 277.

II

INITIATION ANCIENT AND EASTERN

1. Tertullian, *de baptismo*, 18. Origen, *Comm. in Rom.* V, 9.

2. Chapter 21. The latest critical edition is by B. Botte, *La Tradition apostolique de saint Hippolyte; essai de reconstitution*, Münster i. W., 1963. For a detailed account of initiation in the ante-Nicene Church, see my article "The Baptismal Eucharist before Nicaea" in *Studia Liturgica* 4 (1965), pp. 9–36.

3. E.g. (1) Early Syrian tradition knew only one anointing and that was for conferring the Spirit *before* the water baptism (see p. 18 and p. 87, n. 35); (2) After baptism, Africa, Milan, Spain, Gaul and Ireland long had one anointing rather than the two post-baptismal anointings of the Roman practice of the *Apostolic Tradition* and later; no Eastern rite has two distinct ceremonies of post-baptismal unction; (3) In the Coptic, Ethiopic and East Syrian rites, post-baptismal imposition of hands is a ceremony distinct from unction, though this is not the case in the Byzantine, Armenian and West Syrian rites; in the early medieval West the presence of a distinct hand-laying, or its nature (general or individual?), are disputed questions for certain times and places, and its meaning in relation to the meaning of unction is also a matter of discussion; (4) A washing of the candidates' feet, after the pattern of John 13, was firmly established after the post-baptismal anointing in Milan, Gaul and Ireland.

4. Chief among these are: Justin, *Apol.* I, 61; Tertullian, *de baptismo*; Cyril of Jerusalem, *Catecheses;* Ambrose of Milan, *de sacramentis* and *de mysteriis; Apos-*

tolic Constitutions, III, 16ff.; VII, 22; VII, 39ff.; *Pilgrimage of Etheria*; John Chrysostom, *Huit catéchèses baptismales*, first edited by A. Wenger, Paris, 1957; Theodore of Mopsuestia, *Catechetical Homilies*; and the writings of Augustine.

5. That we cannot be sure that the whole of this rite goes back much beyond the last decades of the second century is due to the fact that Justin Martyr, writing about 150, makes no mention of those ceremonies which eventually formed the detached rite of confirmation in the West, even though in other respects he gives an outline of the service corresponding closely to that of the *Apostolic Tradition.* The times and places of the introduction of anointing and hand-laying are the object of much speculation.

6. At the stage of their proximate preparation the catechumens were called *electi* at Rome, *competentes* elsewhere in the West, and φωτιζόμενοι in the East.

7. This proximate preparation for baptism is the origin of Lent, a season whose length varied according to time and place. We know from later evidence that various ceremonies took place at different points in Lent, such as the *traditio* and *redditio* of the Creed.

8. This may have been a general extension of the hand over them all (as in the present Roman rite of confirmation), rather than an individual imposition on each. See pp. 188f. of T. Marsh, "The History and Significance of the Post-baptismal Rites" in *Irish Theological Quarterly* 29 (1962).

9. The versions reveal a difference concerning the moment of the Spirit's reception. Lampe (*The Seal of the Spirit*, pp. 136–48) preferred the Latin version: "O Lord God, who didst count these worthy of deserving the forgiveness of sins by the laver of regeneration of the Holy Spirit, send upon them Thy grace that they may serve Thee according to Thy will . . ." Dix preferred the Oriental: "O Lord God, who didst count these worthy of deserving the forgiveness of sins by the laver of regeneration, make them worthy to be filled with Thy Holy Spirit and send upon them Thy grace. . . ." B. Botte has now transferred his favours to the Oriental versions (see pp. 52f. of his latest edition, 1963); see also J. Crehan, "The Sealing at Confirmation" in *Theological Studies* 14 (1953), pp. 273–9.

10. Almost certainly referring to the tracing of the sign of the cross; cf. Tertullian, *Adv. Marc.* III, 22 and *De res. carn.*, 8.

11. For the milk and honey cf. Clement of Alexandria, *Paed.* I, 6 and 34ff.; Tertullian, *Adv. Marc.*, I, 14 and *De cor. mil.*, 3. See also J. Crehan, *Early Christian Baptism and the Creed*, London, 1950, pp. 171–75.

12. Apart, that is, from some European and a few (rather "high church") British Baptist congregations in which baptism is immediately followed by a hand-laying and communion.

13. The Coptic rite is translated in R. M. Woolley, *Coptic Offices*, London, 1930, and additional information is found in O. H. E. Burmester, "The Baptismal Rite of the Coptic Church (A Critical Study)" in *Bulletin de la Société d'Archéologie copte* 11 (1945), Cairo, 1947, pp. 27–86 and in M. de Fénoyl, "Les

sacrements de l'initiation chrétienne dans l'Eglise copte" in *Proche-Orient Chrétien* 7 (1957), pp. 7–25. The Ethiopian rite is found in S. Grébaut, "Ordre du baptême et de la confirmation dans l'Eglise éthiopienne" in *Revue de l'Orient chrétien* 26 (1927–8), pp. 105–89.

14. The infant's sponsor speaks for him.

15. A theological commentary on another Oriental rite, the West Syrian, is given from within the Jacobite tradition in India in an article by P. Verghese in *Studia Liturgica*, 4 (1965), pp. 81–93.

16. As late as 1932 the Roman Congregation of the Sacraments gave a much qualified permission for the continuance of the ancient practice of giving confirmation to infants immediately after their baptism in Spain and parts of Latin America. I gather, however, that the custom has now practically died out.

17. *Baptism in the New Testament*, pp. 364–67.

18. It may be that the revised rite of infant baptism promised by the *De Liturgia* of Vatican II will touch on this point: "Ritus baptizandi parvulos recognoscatur et verae infantium condicioni accommodetur" (§67).

19. This is an accusation which the Church of Scotland's 1955 Interim Report (p. 20) makes against the Baptist movement.

20. The Greek rite, for example, indicates that a sponsor shall speak in cases where "the candidate is a barbarian or a child".

21. Expressed in *Von der Wiedertaufe*, 1528, Weimar edition, vol. 26, pp. 156, 169.

22. See E. C. Whitaker, "The Baptismal Interrogations" in *Theology* 59 (1956), pp. 103–12. Whitaker also points out that some eleventh-century MSS of the Spanish *Liber Ordinum* have the response "He shall believe".

23. ". . . Wherefore, after this promise made by Christ, this infant must also faithfully, for his part, promise by you that are his sureties (until he come of age to take it upon himself) that he will renounce the devil and all his works, and constantly believe God's holy Word, and obediently keep his commandments.

I demand therefore,

Dost thou, in the name of this Child, renounce . . . ?"

This text clearly shows that the relation between baptism and the faith of the candidate was recognized to be a problem in the case of infant baptism; and a brave attempt has been made, in the notion of *temporary substitution*, to solve the problem in a way which both brings a faith which is present and personal (i.e. belonging to the candidate) into play at the actual baptism and yet also acknowledges that the child's own faith is in some sense still in the future. But can there really be, however temporarily, this kind of substitution ("This infant must promise by you . . ." and "Dost thou, in the name of this child, renounce . . . ?") when personal salvation is at stake? The cases are not parallel, but the embarrassment which commentators experience at the suggestion that Paul might have countenanced "baptism for the dead" (1 Cor. 15: 29) at least prompts the thought that the matter is open to grave theological doubt.

24. E.g. the Methodist *Book of Offices*, London, 1936; the *Liturgie de l'Eglise de Genève*, 1945; the Congregationalist *Book of Services and Prayers*, Independent Press, London, 1959.

25. No negative conclusion is to be drawn from this concerning the eternal destiny of a baptized infant who dies before being of an age to profess faith.

26. In some Protestant circles there is a danger of attaching such great importance to the later profession of faith in the making of a Christian that the act of God at the distant moment of an infant baptism is forgotten.

27. Anglican confirmation services include both a profession of faith by the candidates and also the hand-laying by the bishop. The Roman Catholic theologian Suarez (+1617) gives as one reason for preferring the postponement of confirmation until the age of reason the fact that the reception of the sacrament may then be viewed as a personal profession of faith ("Praeterea, cum in hoc sacramento fiat veluti secunda professio fidei, per se videtur expediens, cum prima in baptismo facta sit per alios, ut secunda in hoc sacramento fiat per ipsum et suscipientem"; *Opera omnia*, vol. 20, Paris, 1860, pp. 669f.). The *Constitutio de Sacra Liturgia* of Vatican II speaks of the suitability of a *renovatio promissionum baptismi* preceding confirmation (§71). It is doubtful whether this aspect of confirmation at least is of much value when the confirmand has already professed his faith at his adult baptism.

28. Among the Copts a custom persists whereby at this feast the faithful plunge into a large bowl of water which has been blessed by the priest; see p. 19 of the article by M. de Fénoyl mentioned on p. 89, note 13.

29. *Baptism in the New Testament*, pp. 29f.

30. The reasons advanced by the Church of Scotland's 1958 *Biblical Doctrine of Baptism* (pp. 30–32, 54) will hardly bear looking at: (i) in baptism we are (entirely) passive but in the Lord's Supper we are (also) active ("This *do* . . .") in a way in which an infant cannot be—but this is completely to ignore the *active* baptismal aorists of Gal. 5: 24 or Col. 3: 9; (ii) God accommodates His action towards us "as we are able to receive it" and it is (apparently) He who has determined that infants may be baptized but not yet receive communion—but this is a most blatant *deus ex machina* solution; (iii) it is apparently part of the "divine self-accommodation" to our weakness that "our incorporation into Christ" may take place at our baptism as infants but that "the insertion of Christ into us" then waits for several years until first communion—but this is to make the Lord responsible for driving an intolerable wedge between our life in Christ and Christ's life in us. The Church of Scotland has, however, at least tried to justify a practice which several other denominations less thinkingly share.

31. P. G. Bretscher, "First Things First: The Question of Infant Communion", in *Una Sancta* 30 (1962), pp. 34–40.

III

INITIATION MEDIEVAL AND WESTERN

1. See the surveys in J. D. C. Fisher, *Christian Initiation–Baptism in the Medieval West*, London, 1965; T. Marsh, "The history and significance of the post-baptismal rites", in *Irish Theological Quarterly* 29 (1962), pp. 175–206; and D. van den Eynde, "Les rites liturgiques latins de la confirmation", in *La Maison–Dieu*, no. 54 (1958), pp. 53–78.

2. See the *Apostolic Tradition*, and the letter of Innocent of Rome to Decentius of Gubbio in the year 416 (Ep. 25, PL 56, 515). In the history of the rite of confirmation the Roman trend has been to maximize the anointing and consignation and minimize the hand-laying. But the imposition of hands has never been wholly lost sight of, thanks no doubt to the recurrent influence of Acts 8: 17 and 19: 6.

3. See J. D. C. Fisher, whose reconstruction is probable but not indisputable.

4. See, e.g., B. Neunheuser, *Taufe und Firmung*, Freiburg i. B., 1956.

5. This restriction need not be seen simply as a piece of self-assertive prelacy on the part of the episcopate: it served to secure that a part should be played in the initiation ceremonies by one who was viewed as a guardian of the Church's *unity*. Already Ignatius of Antioch made the following requirement for the avoidance of divisions: "Let no man perform anything pertaining to the Church without the bishop. . . . It is not permitted to baptize . . . apart from the bishop. But whatever he may approve, that is well-pleasing to God . . ." (*Ad. Smyrn.*, 8). The East chose another way than the Roman; presbyters were allowed to administer the whole rite of initiation, but used episcopally or even patriarchally consecrated *myron* for the post-baptismal chrismation.

6. The Papal Decree of 1946 which empowers the parish priest, as "extraordinary minister", to confirm in a case of emergency appears to have the grudging support of Gregory the Great in Roman history (Ep. 26, PL 77, 696; cf. St Thomas, S.T. III, 72, 11).

7. For the literature, see above, p. 16.

8. Lampe's position is clearly that contained in the plain words of the Prayer Book ("Give thy Holy Spirit to this infant, that he may be born again . . ."), and he quotes Jewel, Barrow and Beveridge among older writers as teaching that the Spirit is sacramentally bestowed in baptism (see *The Seal of the Spirit*, especially pp. 312–15).

9. See Article XXV of the XXXIX Articles of the Church of England.

10. The Prayer Book service talks of the candidates *being confirmed* and also of their "ratifying and *confirming*" the baptismal promise and vow.

11. *Greek Baptismal Terminology: its origins and early development*, Nijmegen, 1962.

12. The distinction made by some Anglican scholars between an "external operation" of the Spirit at water baptism (for regeneration and the remission of sins) and the "gift of the indwelling Spirit" in the post-baptismal ceremonies introduces an artificial enough distinction in the role of the Spirit in salvation; but its artificiality is even surpassed by this distinction of Ysebaert's. How far it departs from biblical reality will be gauged from the difficulties Ysebaert has with Rom. 8: 9–11 (p. 270).

13. Ysebaert sets great store by certain recurrent phrases in the New Testament (chiefly (*a*) βαπτίζειν (ἐν) πνεύματι ἁγίῳ, and (*b*) τὸ πνεῦμα ἐκχειν, τὸ π. διδόναι, τὸ π. λαμβάνειν, and ἡ δωρεὰ τοῦ ἁγίου πνεύματος) which he believes to have been already part of an "established linguistic usage" for a post-baptismal rite by which the Spirit was given; these phrases are then used as a talisman in the interpretation of patristic texts. In fact, however, the basic N.T. case for this determinative meaning is very weak: (*a*) For his distinction between baptism in water and "baptism in the Holy Spirit" Ysebaert relies on Matt. 3: 11, Mark 1: 8, Luke 3: 16, John 1: 26ff., Acts 1: 5; 11: 16; but in each of these cases the water baptism is *John's*, and these instances therefore tell in no way against the view that in *Christian* baptism the water and the Spirit are normally the outside and the inside of a single event; (*b*) Acts 8: 17; 19: 6 look good, provided these episodes are taken as normal rather than as exceptional: but for further support of his association of τὸ πνεῦμα ἐκχεῖν, διδόναι, λαμβάνειν with a post-baptismal ceremony Ysebaert is driven to such desperate exegesis as the following: the whole of Tit. 3: 5 is taken to refer to the "operation" of the Spirit at baptism, while οὗ ἐξέχεεν ἐφ' ἡμᾶς πλουσίως of verse 6 is referred to a separate post-baptismal "gift" (p. 135); in Rom. 5:5 the outpouring of God's love is taken as an "operation" of the Spirit at baptism, while τοῦ δοθέντος ἡμῖν is referred to a different occasion on which the Spirit was "given" (p. 269).

14. That there are sometimes downright inconsistencies in patristic utterances about the moment of the Spirit's reception is plain; but the charge of muddle-headedness against the Fathers can be reduced if the following factors be allowed to account for a certain amount of variety: an effect may be ascribed to one particular ceremony in the whole complex *pars pro toto*; the Fathers' explanations of the initiation complex are often governed by pedagogical aims rather than by the desire to make a strict doctrinal definition; much depends on which biblical passage, and particularly which O.T. type, it is that the Fathers are treating in connection with the baptismal rite.

15. *Principles of Sacramental Theology* (2nd ed.), London, 1960, pp. 162–223.

16. Leeming argues that the Fathers associate the vocabulary of "perfecting", "completing" and "fulfilling" especially with the "confirmation" part of the baptismal complex. Fisher argues (pp. 141–48) that the word *confirmare* itself

was used in this sense before coming to be understood primarily as "strengthen".

17. The defining of confirmational character has been an embarrassment to Roman Catholic theologians. Leeming says that the confirmational character gives a share in the *apostolic* work of the Church, a commissioning to confess Christ officially and publicly (see Thomas, S.T. III, 72, 5). True, this means a sharing in "Christ's Mediatorial office of bringing the truth and charity of God to others" (p. 238); but some Roman Catholic theologians hold that the special participation in Christ's priesthood which is their agreed meaning of sacramental character demands, in the case of confirmation just as much as in baptism and orders, expression in the *liturgical* life of the Church. It will be seen below that L. Bouyer and B. Luykx argue that confirmation confers a certain status in eucharistic worship: it gives a person power to participate fully within the offering and receiving people of God at mass. In practice, however, Roman Catholicism does not demand a person to be confirmed before he may have full lay participation in the eucharist: baptism suffices for that.

18. A further difficulty for many Protestants in the way in which Leeming presents his case will be the distinction between the validity of a sacrament and its efficacy or fruitfulness which is involved in the distinction between seal (=character) and gift.

19. See, e.g., the issues of the periodicals *La Maison-Dieu* (no. 54; 1958) and *Lumière et Vie* (no. 51; 1961) devoted to confirmation.

20. It is ascribed to Eusebius of Emesa in M. de la Bigne: *Magna Bibliotheca Veterum Patrum*, vol. 5, Coloniae Agrippinae, 1618, pp. 571f.

21. "Que signifie la confirmation?" in *Paroisse et Liturgie*, 34 (1952), pp. 3–12, 65–67; cf. B. Luykx, "Théologie et pastorale de la confirmation" in *Paroisse et Liturgie*, 39 (1957), pp. 180–201, 263–78.

22. E.g. A. G. Martimort, "La Confirmation" in the composite volume *Communion solennelle et profession de foi*, Paris, 1952 (series *Lex Orandi*, 14), pp. 159–201; T. Marsh, "Confirmation in its relation to Baptism" in *Irish Theological Quarterly* 27 (1960), pp. 259–93; C. Davis, *The Making of a Christian*, London, 1964, chapter 5.

23. Tertullian, *De res. carn.*, 8 (PL 2,806); Cyril, *Myst. Cat.*, III, 4.

24. *De cler. inst.* I, 30 (PL 107, 314).

25. Cyril, *Myst. Cat.*, III; *Apostolic Constitutions*, VII, 44, 2 (ed. F. X. Funk, I, p. 450); Theodoret, *In Cant. Cant.*, 1, 2 (PG 81, 57–60); also St Thomas, S.T. III, 72, 2.

26. Acts 1: 8; 2: 1–11; 4: 31.

27. The *De Liturgia* of Vatican II now mentions the suitability of confirmation's being preceded by a renewal of baptismal vows. It remains to be seen whether the promised revision of the confirmation rite will actually include a profession of faith.

28. In *Die Geschichte der Konfirmation* (1958) the Swiss Reformed L. Vischer presents a historical sketch of confirmation in the Reformed, and indeed the

Lutheran, traditions. He shows how in the course of the centuries since the Reformation various ideas have attached themselves to a ceremony which has itself taken various forms: "confirmation" has involved (in varying combinations) instruction and examination in the faith, personal conversion, admission to communion, entry into adult society, blessing of or intercession for the candidate.

29. Thurian entitles his study: *La Confirmation: consécration des laïcs* (Neuchâtel/Paris, 1957).

30. "La Confirmation" in his volume of essays *Prophétisme sacramentel*, Neuchâtel, 1964, pp. 141–82.

31. So the Reformed, G. Deluz, "Le baptême d'eau et d'Esprit ou le problème de la confirmation" in *Etudes théologiques et religieuses* (Montpellier), 22 (1947), pp. 201–35.

32. So the Pietists.

33. Document 16 of the Assembly. The German original should be read: the official E.T. is unreliable.

34. K. Frör (ed.), *Confirmatio—Forschungen zur Geschichte und Praxis der Konfirmation*, München, 1959.

35. K. Frör (ed.), *Zur Geschichte und Ordnung der Konfirmation in den Lutherischen Kirchen*, München, 1962.

36. Though Luther was prepared to call confirmation a *ceremonia sacramentalis*, this expression should not be overestimated; for Luther rejected confirmation as a sacrament in the proper sense because it lacked Dominical institution. Bucer also ranked confirmation (*Handauﬄegen*) merely among the "sakramentliche Ceremonien" but even so used the formula "Nim hin den heiligen geist . . ." at the imposition of hands in the order of confirmation in the *Casseler Kirchenordnung* of 1539.

37. I take my information from the most widely used service book in English Congregationalism: *A Book of Services and Prayers*, published by the Independent Press, London, 1959.

38. See *The Book of Offices*, Methodist Publishing House, London, 1936. (A thorough revision of the Book of Offices is being undertaken.)

39. Bouyer and his supporters have to make use of the notion of a "votum Confirmationis" implicit in baptism.

40. *Directoire de la pastorale des sacrements*, 1951.

41. Though they practise early confirmation and communion, the French themselves have the so-called *communion solennelle*, preceded by the *profession de foi*, at about the age of twelve; this occasion apparently has its roots in parish missions of the seventeenth century.

42. So, e.g., von Allmen.

43. So the main thrust of Heubach's L.W.F. document.

44. So Thurian.

45. In English Methodism and Congregationalism, communion is often

administered to young people before they have been received as "members", though no minister would give communion to a child who had not received some instruction in the faith and shown some sign of personal belief. (The *de facto* anticipation of that "reception into full communion upon profession of faith" which the Membership Service is supposed to embody is occasioned by the practice of delaying "membership" (which also implies certain *governmental* functions in the Church) until the later teens.)

46. It is not sufficient to talk, as Thurian does, of the need to "discern the body". If faith is assumed to be present, whether actually, vicariously or proleptically, at the baptism of an infant, then similar assumptions are also applicable in the case of "discerning the body" at communion.

47. The Roman Catholics let the whole *liturgical* catechumenate precede infant baptism, but the real instruction is of course postponed till the age of reason.

48. Since the catechumenate may (indeed should) stretch over a considerable period, there is nothing against its being *started* in infancy with an "admission to the catechumenate" (see 78 f.).

49. As K. Barth.

IV

BELIEVERS' BAPTISM

1. *Comm. in Rom.*, V. 9 (PG 14, 1047), written at Caesarea.

2. *Ep.* 64 (Vienna corpus).

3. Acts 16: 15; 16: 31–34; 18: 8; 1 Cor. 1: 16.

4. *Baptism in the New Testament*, pp. 71–80.

5. Interim Report, 1955, p. 28.

6. 1 Apol. 15, written about 150; cf. the use of the verb at Matt. 28: 19.

7. *Mart. Polyc.*, 9 (PG 5, 1036).

8. J. Jeremias, *Die Kindertaufe in den ersten vier Jahrhunderten*, Göttingen, 1958; revised in E. T. *Infant Baptism in the First Four Centuries*, London, 1960; also *Nochmals: Die Anfänge der Kindertaufe*, München, 1962; E.T., *The Origins of Infant Baptism: a further study in reply to Kurt Aland*, London, 1963. K. Aland, *Die Säuglingstaufe im Neuen Testament und in der alten Kirche*, München, 1961; E.T., *Did the early Church baptize infants?*, London, 1963.

9. *The Unity of the Bible*, London, 1953, ch. VI.

10. *Baptism in the New Testament*, pp. 152–60, 334–44; also in *Christian Baptism*, ed. A. Gilmore, pp. 139–41.

11. That there are both similarities and differences is to be seen in the light of the fact that there is both continuity and discontinuity between the Old Covenant and the New Covenant inaugurated by the *death* of Jesus.

12. *Die Taufe—Ein Sakrament?*, Zollikon-Zürich, 1951, pp. 155–7.

13. Cf. Hebrews 6: 1–6 and 10: 26.

14. E.g., Greg. Nyss., *Adversus eos qui differunt baptismum* (PG 46, 416–32); Basil, *Hom. 13, Exhort. ad sanctum baptisma* (PG 31, 424–44).

15. See their document, *The Key of Truth*, ed. and tr. F. C. Conybeare, Oxford, 1898.

16. The name appears to be Zwingli's dubbing, used in the title of his work, *Von dem touff, von widertouff unnd vom Kindertouff*, which was written in May 1525, four months after Grebel and Blaurock had performed the first re-baptisms.

17. A denomination originating in America in the nineteenth century.

18. E.T., *The Divine-Human Encounter*, London, 1944.

19. *Die Taufe im Neuen Testament*, Stuttgart, 1952; and *Taufe und Gemeinde im Neuen Testament*, Kassel, 1956; E.T., *Baptism and Church in the New Testament*, London, 1957.

20. Ed. A. Gilmore, London, 1959, with the subtitle, *A Fresh Attempt to Understand the Rite in terms of Scripture, History, and Theology*.

21. *De baptismo*, 18.

22. The phrase is from the London Confession of Faith, 1660.

23. *The New Testament Doctrine of Baptism*, p. 135.

24. *Christian Baptism*, p. 313.

25. See the brilliant study by the Dutch Dominican, E. Schillebeeckx, *Christus, Sacrament van de Godsontmoeting*; E.T., *Christ the Sacrament of Encounter with God*, London and New York, 1963.

26. *Christian Baptism*, p. 308.

27. These are both aorists, representing a single event in the past: baptism.

28. The fact that some British Baptist scholars are now prepared to countenance other modes than complete submersion should not, however, be taken as indicating a general opinion of Baptists, particularly not in the U.S.A.

29. See the Catechetical Orations of Theodore of Mopsuestia (ed. Tonneau, pp. 403, 441–3) and Chrysostom (ed. Wenger, p. 147); but see also Stenzel's arguments on p. 14 above. Thomas Aquinas (S.T. III, 66, 7f.) commends immersion: both single and triple are lawful; the former signifies the oneness of Christ's death, and of the Godhead, while the latter signifies the three days of Christ's burial, and also the three Persons of the Trinity.

30. Permitted as a makeshift by the *Didache*, 7, and now the most frequent use in the Roman, Lutheran and Anglican denominations.

31. Sprinkling is discouraged in the Roman Catholic Church but widely used in the Reformed tradition.

32. This presupposes that parents whose children receive baptism are themselves already Christian. The question of defining such "Christian parents" will be discussed in chapter VI.

33. Acts 2: 39 says nothing direct on infant baptism; but, whether τέκνα

refers to the very children of those who are listening or to their coming generations, the verse shows that the New Covenant did not disregard the family pattern in its promise. 1 Cor. 7: 14 can be manipulated in so many directions that its place in any argument is suspect.

34. The phrase is Clark's, in *Christian Baptism*, p. 321.

35. As maintained by R. E. O. White in *Christian Baptism*, p. 103.

36. As advocated by N. Clark in *Christian Baptism*, pp. 322–23.

37. It is a deep-rooted Christian instinct that parents should want their children acknowledged as closely associated with themselves in God's plan of salvation. The Paulicians had a service for "the giving of a name to the catechumen" eight days after birth, in which God was asked to bless the child and "bring him through to reach holy baptism" (*The Key of Truth*, p. 90f.); and modern Baptists are often driven to hold services of "dedication" or "blessing".

38. For emphatic advocacy of infant baptism on the basis of Covenantal theology, see the work of the Reformed, P. C. Marcel, *Le Baptême, sacrament de l'Alliance de grâce*, in *La Revue Réformée*, 1950; E.T., *The Biblical Doctrine of Infant Baptism*, London, 1953.

39. Neville Clark, unlike some of his more militant forefathers and contemporaries, is unwilling to give an unqualified dismissal to infant baptism as "no baptism" (*Christian Baptism*, p. 325).

V

INITIATION AND UNITY

1. The context makes it quite clear that by "one baptism" the apostle here means the *one-and-the-same* baptism which Christians have in common; he is saying nothing directly about the issue of whether baptism is *one-and-unrepeatable;* nor will this particular phrase here bear all the weight J. A. T. Robinson placed upon it in his thesis, admirable in many respects, propounded in the article cited on p. 86, n. 10.

2. See, e.g., the contribution of T. F. Torrance, "Eschatology and the Eucharist", to D. Baillie and J. Marsh (ed.), *Intercommunion*, London, 1952, especially pp. 339f.

3. Published in *One Lord, One Baptism*, S.C.M. Studies in Ministry and Worship, London, 1960.

4. Despite the warning Baptists had given at the Faith and Order Conference at Edinburgh in 1937, as mentioned above on p. 46.

5. This was already Tertullian's view of heretical baptism (*De bapt.*, 15, PL 1, 1216). The whole material for the controversy about Novatianist baptism is found in Cyprian's Letters 69–75 (Vienna Corpus numbering), and in the anonymous *De rebaptismate*.

6. So Stephen's position is reported by Firmilian (Cyprian, *Ep.* 75). B. Leeming suggests (*Principles of Sacramental Theology*, pp. 189–93) that this is a misrepresentation of Stephen's position due to the fact that Cyprian and Firmilian never grasped that in refusing to (re)baptize converted heretics or schismatics Stephen was already acting, even if he did not advance the argument in so many words, upon an "Augustinian" distinction (see below) between validity and fruitfulness.

7. This second view claims support from Stephen's reported pronouncement: "Si qui ergo a quacumque haeresi veniant ad vos, nihil innovetur nisi quod traditum est, ut manus illis imponatur *in paenitentiam*" (Cyprian, *Ep.* 74).

8. As to the *validity* of schismatic baptism, Augustine maintains throughout that baptism given in schism is still "the baptism of Christ" and is not to be repeated when a person comes from schism to the Catholic Church. As to schismatic baptism's being *inefficacious*, it is true that Augustine is prepared to countenance (*De Baptismo contra Donatistas* I, capp. 11f., PL 43, 118–20; III, cap. 13, PL 43, 146), for the sake of argument, the possibility that remission of sins may be given in such baptism "by virtue of the holiness of baptism (*per baptismi sanctitatem*)" (though in that case baptism would be efficacious, Augustine holds, only at the very moment of administration, since persistence in schism would mean that a man's sins returned upon him immediately); but the other argumentative possibility, namely that baptism in schism is *not efficacious at all* (not even momentarily) until an eventual reconciliation with the Catholic Church, is certainly the view which Augustine himself prefers, as is made clear by his statements elsewhere that there can be no remission of sins outside the Catholic Church to which the Holy Spirit confines His presence (see *Serm.* 71, capp. 17–23, PL 38, 460–66; cf. *Serm.* 8, cap. 11, PL 38, 72f.; *Serm.* 269, PL 38, 1234–7).

9. The notion of a valid but inefficacious baptism seems to stand closer to a conception of the sacrament as the mechanical imposition of an indelible mark and a conception of grace as a (possibly latent) stuff than to the conception of the sacrament as a gracious personal encounter between God and man.

10. In the East a system developed whereby converts were received into communion in differing ways according to the error from which they came: some were received simply upon a profession of the true faith; others were required to be chrismated as well; of yet others baptism itself was required (see Basil, *Ep.* 188, 1, PG 32, 664–72; Timothy of Constantinople, *De Receptione Haereticorum*, PG 86, 10–74; Council in Trullo, canon 95, on which see C. J. von Hefele, *Conciliengeschichte*, vol. 3 (2nd edition, 1877), p. 342; also the Roman Gregory the Great, *Ep.* XI, 67, PL 77, 1204–8).

11. Till the end of the twelfth century the scholastics recognized a baptismal formula "in the name of Jesus" provided it were not used with bad intent in preference to the Trinitarian formula. Pope Nicholas I (858–67) appears to have

accepted "in the name of the Holy Trinity" and "in the name of Christ" as equivalent baptismal formulae, claiming the support of Ambrose (see *De Spir. Sanct.* I, 3, 42, PL 16, 713f.) for this (*Responsa ad consulta Bulgarorum*, 104; PL 119, 1014f.) Thomas Aquinas held that baptism "in the name of Christ" was performed in the primitive Church by virtue of a special revelation given to the apostles (S.T. III, 66, 6). Modern Roman theologians explain that the references in *Acts* to baptism "in the name of (the Lord) Jesus (Christ)" do not reveal a *liturgical formula* but serve to distinguish Christian baptism from John's.

12. This is so generously interpreted that even a pagan may be included. But an Anglican clergyman may be excluded! At least since the Gorham judgment of 1850 some Romans have had doubts about Anglican baptisms, fearing lest the sacrament should have been invalidated by insufficiency of intention on the part of a minister who willed to exclude regeneration from baptism. In consequence, they have frequently had recourse to administering conditional baptism, a practice known to the Western Church since the eighth century (see no. 28 of the second collection of *Statutes of St. Boniface* in C. J. von Hefele, *Conciliengeschichte*, vol. 3, Freiburg i. B., 1877 (2nd edition), p. 585) and to the East since the fourth century (see the *Canonical Responses* of Timothy of Alexand ria,in J. B. Pitra, *Juris ecclesiastici Graecorum historia et monumenta*, Romae, 1864, p. 638) but now rarely used by any apart from Roman Catholics, to converts from Anglicanism ("If thou art not already baptized, I baptize thee . . ."). The shock which this can cause to an ecumenically sensitive generation was shown in the furore provoked by the case of the American President Johnson's daughter in July 1965; the Roman priest who gave her conditional baptism when she had already received Episcopalian baptism did in fact suffer a rebuke from the Roman Secretariat for Christian Unity. A similar outcry had in 1964 accompanied the case of the Dutch Princess Irene who had already been baptized in the Reformed Church.

13. This depends on how far the Orthodox faithful who is allowed to receive Catholic communion and the Orthodox priest from whom a Catholic may now, in certain circumstances, receive communion are considered as *individual separated Catholics* and how far as *members of separated Churches.*

13. I deal here only with the attitude of the Chalcedonian Orthodox to the Western Churches: there is no room to examine the relations between the Chalcedonian Orthodox and the non-Chalcedonian "Orthodox" or between the latter and Catholics or Protestants.

15. See T. Ware, *Eustratios Argenti*, Oxford, 1964, p. 84.

16. See also his *Baptism in the New Testament*, pp. 387–95.

17. This unguarded permission is clearly present in the implications which the committee declares the statement quoted above to entail: "Should *any member* [my italics] of the United Church feel convinced of the necessity for Believers' Baptism he shall be free to seek it. . . . All ministers of the United Church shall be free to administer either or both forms of Baptism."

18. The debate within the Negotiating and Continuation Committees has been accompanied by articles in the quarterly publication of the Negotiating Committee *Church Union News and Views*.

19. In the North India scheme it is the Anglicans, with outside support from the Lutherans, who have argued most strongly against a thing which they would consider rebaptism but which Baptists would consider the first true baptism.

20. "Second Baptism as a case of Conscience" in *Church Union News and Views*, May 1964, pp. 24f.

21. Hindley guards against the possibility of repeated recourse to further baptisms whenever emotional fervour wanes by pointing out that his envisaged "second baptism" takes place only within the complex of initiation which, once totally completed, is strictly unrepeatable.

22. See, e.g., John of Damascus, *De Fid. Orth.*, IV, 9, PG 94, 1120.

23. The Methodist Covenant Service is a particularly solemn occasion for the expression of repeated post-baptismal *metanoia* in a way which does not question but rather explicitly presupposes God's faithfulness to His part of the covenant. On the history and theology of the service, see D. H. Tripp, *The Renewal of the Covenant in the Methodist Tradition*, London, 1968.

24. Though see the Coptic practice mentioned above on p. 91, note 28. A rite (found in J. Goar, *Euchologion sive Rituale Graecorum*, editio secunda, Venetiis, 1730, p. 689) for the reconciliation of apostates, ascribed to Methodius, Patriarch of Constantinople 843–7, includes a washing (λουέσθω) which seems to be intended as a *reminder* of baptism (see M. Jugie, *Theologia Dogmatica Christianorum orientalium*, III, Parisiis, 1930, pp. 145f.). It must be admitted that a few Pentecostalist churches give a fresh baptism to excommunicated members "desiring to refellowship" (see N. Bloch-Hoell, *The Pentecostalist Movement*, Oslo/London, 1964, p. 165). The monastic profession has sometimes been viewed as a "second baptism", but this in a clearly derivative sense. On the Western *Asperges* before Sunday mass, see B. Fischer, "Formes de la commémoration du baptême en Occident" in *La Maison-Dieu*, no. 58 (1959), pp. 111–34, in particular pp. 119–21.

25. The *Statement of Convictions* issued in 1965 by the Joint Committee for Conversations between the Congregational Union of England and Wales and the Presbyterian Church of England declares that unbaptized members of the uniting denominations might be accepted as members in the new Church (this is presumably a concession by the Presbyterians to some Congregationalists), provided that all *future* members of the united Church will be baptized. In this case, unbaptized members are a temporary irregularity: there is no thought of allowing a continuing witness to the dispensability of baptism.

VI

INITIATION AND MISSION

1. We try to use "baptism" and "the Church" in this chapter in a way which depends as little as possible on the answers given to the questions posed on p. 58. above.

2. A. Schmemann, *For the Life of the World*, New York, 1963, p. 47.

3. See P. Evdokimov, *L'Orthodoxie*, Neuchâtel/Paris, 1959, pp. 277–87.

4. *Dial. contra Lucif.*, 4, PL 23, 158.

5. In Protestantism the "State Churches" and *Volkskirchen* know most acutely the problem of the non-practising baptized, whether in England, Scotland, Scandinavia or West Germany. (In present-day England some 27 million people have been baptized in the Anglican Church, some 10 million have been confirmed, and the number of communicants at Easter, the sole day of obligation in the Church of England, is 2¼ million.) A similar phenomenon is observable in large areas of "de-christianization" in predominantly Roman Catholic countries of Europe and Latin America.

6. Freytag has a number of essays on the sacraments on the mission field in his collected *Reden und Aufsätze*, I (ed. J. Hermelink and H. J. Margull), München, 1961. See also G. F. Vicedom, *Die Taufe unter den Heiden*, München, 1960.

7. *Das Taufproblem in der Mission*, Gütersloh, 1951, pp. 62–7.

8 *Acts of Paul and Thecla*, 34.

9. This is not to say that baptismal practice is perfect in these situations: (1) In the case of family baptisms one member, usually the grandmother, may abstain in order to secure for the family the benefits of the old religion to which the baptized have no access. (2) The younger churches have not always been quick to act upon the obligation to mission which baptism lays on them (though Bishop Azariah of Dornakal, so he told the meeting of the International Missionary Council at Tambaram in 1938, used to tour the churches and have the baptized members place their hands upon their heads and declare "I am a baptized Christian. Woe unto me if I preach not the Gospel.") (3) In India, an adult convert baptized in a "mass movement" may be required to spend years *after his baptism* in attaining a higher standard of piety or of Christian knowledge before he is "confirmed" and admitted to the Lord's Supper. Yet positive contributions are already being made by the Church in a heathen-mission situation: it was, for instance, chiefly as a result of pressure from these lands that the Roman Catholic Church reintroduced in 1962 a liturgical catechumenate for adult converts in which ceremony and instruction go hand in hand throughout the period of preparation for baptism. Perhaps also we may look to the African awareness of the power of "spirit" for help in making explicit once more the

Pneumatological reference of baptism which often remains unsung in the West, and to the African grasp of the dwelling together of many people in one corporate whole for a renewal of our understanding of the ecclesiological reference of baptism.

10. For the (Protestant) Church in East Germany I draw most of my information from a lecture delivered to the Faith and Order Commission of the World Council of Churches at St. Andrews in 1960 by Dr G. Jacob of Berlin on "Problems of Baptismal Practice in Areas under Communist Rule Today" (the E.T. is published in Faith and Order Paper No. 31, pp. 49–56); this paper is supplemented from more recent private sources.

11. Jacob argued against the adoption of this policy on the ground that the communist ceremonies are incompatible with Christian baptism. He quoted from a document on the socialist ceremonies, published in Stalinstadt: "The working class and their Party, taking their stand on the ideology of dialectic materialism, and with the help of the Socialist state, are beginning to celebrate birth, marriage and death as events in the life of the emerging Socialist society. These ceremonies are based on Socialist humanism, which is atheistic and does not recognize any higher nature for mankind." In the ceremony the parents take this vow, "Recognizing our responsibility to progressive humanity, to ourselves and to our child, we vow to bring up our son/daughter as a citizen who feels, thinks and acts as a Socialist." The name-giving ceremony usually takes place in the "House of Culture" on a Sunday morning, surrounded by floral decoration and vaudeville trappings.

12. De-christianization is affecting the whole of Western Europe, though of course there are differences between Sweden and Spain or between France and Germany. If I concentrate on Britain, it is because this situation is best known to writer and readers alike.

13. Vidler gave this title to an article in *Theology* (41), pp. 1–9.

14. *Theologie der missionarischen Verkündigung: Evangelisation als ökumenisches Problem*, Stuttgart, 1959.

15. This is to borrow the title of the published report (ed. B. S. Moss) of an ecumenical conference organized by the Anglican Parish and People movement in 1965.

16. See his *Receive this child*. London, 1951.

17. See D. Mason (ed.) *News from Notting Hill*, London, 1967, p. 50.

18. In the Roman Catholic *Clergy Review* 48 (1963), pp. 346–52.

19. *Apud* H. Denzinger, *Ritus Orientalium*, Würzburg, 1863, vol. I, p. 280. Augustine also shows that catechumens were called Christians (*In. Jo. Ev. Tract.* 44, 2; PL 35, 1714), and the same is true of canon 39 of the Council of Elvira (*circa* 305) if Hefele's interpretation is correct (*Conciliengeschichte*, Freiburg i.B., 2nd edition 1873, vol. 1, pp. 171–3).

20. PL 40, 637 (for the ascription to Quodvultdeus rather than to Augustine see G. Morin in *Revue Bénédictine* 31 (1914), pp. 156–62): a signing with the

cross was one of the ceremonies of admission to the catechumenate. In his *Confessions* (I, 11), Augustine tells that from birth "signabar signo crucis Eius et condiebar Eius sale" (the "giving of salt" was another of the ceremonies of the catechumenate in Rome and Africa; see A. Stenzel, *Die Taufe*, pp. 171–75), but he was not baptized until he was over thirty.

21. This finds biblical sanction in the Old Testament conception of the name.

22. That the *Adoptionist Paulicians* (see above, p. 98, note 37) had a ceremony for admitting an infant to the catechumenate and bestowing a name on him (reserving baptism for a season which accorded better with their Christology) is no reason, except for the quibbler, against the use of a similar ceremony by the *orthodox* Church today.

23. There is unfortunately a touch of this about the 1955 Anglican Minority Schedule's proposals.

24. In harmony with the decision of the National Synod of 1951, the *Liturgie de l'Eglise Réformée de France* (Paris, 1963) gives a service for the "Présentation ou Bénédiction d'un enfant" which may only be used, so it is made clear, *en vue de son baptême*. In the service, the Church and the parents recognize their responsibility for the child's education so that he may come to know Christ and ask for baptism.

INDEX